LOOKING
BACKWARDS
OVER BURMA

First published in 2009 by

WOODFIELD PUBLISHING LTD
Bognor Regis ~ West Sussex ~ England ~ PO21 5EL
www.woodfieldpublishing.co.uk

ISBN 1-84683-073-7

Looking Backwards Over Burma

*Wartime recollections of a
RAF Beaufighter Navigator*

DENNIS SPENCER DFC

Woodfield

Woodfield Publishing Ltd

Woodfield House ~ Babsham Lane ~ Bognor Regis ~ West Sussex ~ PO21 5EL
telephone 01243 821234 ~ e-mail enquiries@woodfieldpublishing.co.uk

Interesting and informative books on a variety of subjects

For full details of all our published titles, visit our website at
www.woodfieldpublishing.co.uk

for Geoff

Pilot Geoff Vardigans jokes with LAC Mackenzie about a bullet hole in one of the Beaufighter's propellers.

~ CONTENTS ~

Editor's Preface

In this enjoyable and informative military memoir, Dennis Spencer recalls his experiences as an observer/navigator in the two-man crew of a Bristol Beaufighter ~ the twin-engined, long-range, heavy fighter aircraft that served with such distinction in a variety of roles during World War II ~ in which he clocked up over 200 operational hours whilst on active service with 211 Squadron, of 224 Group, Third Tactical Air Force, South East Asia Air Command.

Alongside his flying partner, pilot Geoff Vardigans, Dennis undertook 52 hazardous sorties over Japanese-occupied territory in Burma and Siam (now Myanmar and Thailand) during 1944.[1]

In Beaufighters armed with under-wing rocket projectiles in addition to their usual cannons, the aircrews of 211 Squadron were given the task of seeking out and attacking enemy road, rail and waterborne transport of all kinds, which required them to fly long distances at low level over hostile territory, often for many hours at a stretch, with little hope of escape or rescue in the event of mechanical failure, pilot fatigue or being shot down – all of which were distinct possibilities.

About the only thing in their favour was the Beaufighter's remarkably silent approach at a low level, enabling surprise attacks to be achieved on many occasions and earning the aircraft its macabre nickname *Whispering Death.*

---

[1] Dennis and Geoff were both awarded the Distinguished Flying Cross (DFC) after completing their tour of duty. The citation for Dennis's award reads: *"This officer as navigator has taken part in numerous operational sorties. He has penetrated deep into enemy territory and attacked many well defended targets. At all times he has displayed great keenness and determination and has never let either adverse weather or enemy opposition deter him from completing his missions."*

Flying long-range missions at low level, over hilly jungle terrain, presented numerous challenges to both pilot and navigator and Dennis does well to describe the mixture of excitement and anxiety he experienced on operations, with much of his time spent facing backwards, in the Beaufighter's swivelling navigator's seat, keeping a watchful eye for enemy fighters – hence the doubly apposite title of his memoir.

As readers will discover, Dennis and Geoff were fortunate to complete their tour of duty, a feat they achieved only after surviving several 'close shaves' of one kind or another – including crash landings, mechanical problems, navigational difficulties, adverse weather conditions and, of course, enemy gunfire – all of which, on occasions, brought them perilously close to sharing the fate of their many squadron colleagues who were killed on operations.

Thus Dennis's recollections perform the important dual function of recording for posterity not only his own personal experiences but also the challenges shared by all those aircrews who went into action over the jungles of South East Asia during the penultimate year of World War II.

By doing so, he has given a voice to those who, tragically, did not survive to share in the victory celebrations that took place just a few months later, or the long years of peace that followed – a peace they all played their part in earning.

Acknowledgements

I would like to thank my wife Annabelle for all her help and encouragement.

And my very sincere thanks are also due to the following three people, whom I have never met:

Donald R. Clark, Australia
www.211squadron.org

Miss Eunice Wilson, UK
Private Researcher

Dr Elizabeth Kaegi Dutton
Canada

No.9 OTU Crosby-on-Eden ~ Geoff Vardigans seated second from left, with the Author standing behind him.

Introduction

The Bristol Beaufighter was a very versatile aircraft. During the 1939/45 war it was used not just as a fighter to engage enemy aircraft in combat but also for air-to-ground strafing in a tactical support role. Beaufighters were also used extensively by Coastal Command, both for convoy escort and strikes against enemy shipping. Some of these aircraft, called Torbeaus, were adapted to carry torpedoes. Others were fitted with an air-to-air radar device and were successfully used as night fighters in the defence of Britain and elsewhere.

It was not until towards the end of 1942 that Beaufighters were first used in the Far East, as part of the Third Tactical Air Force. Under 224 Group, three squadrons were re-formed and equipped with Beaufighters, which were successfully used in a long-range, low-level air-to-ground attack role against Japanese rail, road and river transportation. No.27 Squadron effectively began operating in January 1943, from Agatala. They were pioneers in the use of Beaufighters in this theatre for low-level attacks against the invading Japanese forces that were, at the time, sweeping northwards through Burma. This continued until the monsoon rains made flying very hazardous. Later that year, a second squadron, No.177, was equipped and trained in India and began operating in September from Feni. Meanwhile, a third squadron, No.211, was formed, and trained at Silchar. This squadron was equipped with Beaufighter Mk.Xs, adapted to carry eight rocket projectiles slung under the wings, in addition to the normal armament of four 20mm cannons. The squadron began operating from a grass airfield at Bhatpara early in 1944.

The activities of both 27 and 177 Squadrons have been chronicled in two excellent books; the first in *Beaufighters over Burma* by David J. Innes (1985) and the second in *Silently Into the Midst of Things* by Athol Sutherland Brown

(2001). Both these authors were commissioned officers on their respective squadrons. The fact that they were writing long after the events, and when both were domiciled outside the UK, making it difficult to contact former comrades and to consult official records, makes their achievements all the more commendable.

However, with regard to 211 Squadron, I am not aware of anything published about it by anyone who actually served on it during 1944, with the exception of a chapter in *The Long Sunset* by Antony Montague Brown, who was a pilot on the squadron from about November onwards.

I served as a Navigator/W on this squadron with my pilot Geoff (the late Flight Lieutenant G.V. Vardigans, DFC) and together we survived an operational tour of some 52 sorties, mostly long range and at low-level, over Japanese-occupied Burma from April through to December 1944. As was usual after completing a tour, we were split up and sent to different units, on six months rest from operational flying. We might have got together again to do a second tour (probably on Mosquito aircraft, which were replacing the Beaufighter) but VJ day intervened and the war was over.

In the ensuing period, India was awash with redundant aircrew, with nothing to do and all impatient to get back to the UK, but there was not enough air or sea transportation to get them home quickly and some had to wait months. During this period, I was fortunate enough, partly as a result of a stroke of luck, to secure a job flying as a navigator on BAFSEA (British Air Forces, South East Asia) Communications Squadron, stationed at New Delhi. This was a plum job! We flew VIPs to destinations all over India in American Expediters – these were small, twin-engined aircraft, which could carry up to four passengers. It was interesting work, which I continued to enjoy until June 1946, when I was repatriated to the UK. However, during this time I lost contact with Geoff and did not even know his home address.

I returned to civilian life, met and married Annabelle, had two sons and continued my career as a Development Engineer until I retired in 1984. The sometimes traumatic memories of 1944 were buried deep in the recesses of my mind and I didn't think about them much, and certainly had no thoughts of writing about them. But the advent of the 50th anniversary of VJ day, and the reading of Air Commodore Henry Probert's excellent book *The Forgotten Air Force*, which I received as a present, brought many memories flooding back and I decided that I must attempt to write some memoirs for the family.

As a first step, I thought I would try to find out what had happened to Geoff. This proved surprisingly easy. Amongst some old photographs taken by official RAF photographers, which I had purchased from the Imperial War Museum soon after the war, was one of Geoff, surveying a bullet-hole in the propeller of one of our Beaufighters. The caption for this photograph had been on a separate piece of paper, but I eventually found it among some other souvenirs. It stated that Flt/Lt G. Vardigans had lived at Melton Constable, a village in Norfolk only about forty miles from where I was now living in Suffolk. I looked up the telephone directory for the area and found that it listed only five Vardigans. The first one I rang was his brother!

Sadly, I learned that Geoff had died in 1981. I had moved to Suffolk in 1965 and now regret that I had not tried to trace him earlier. It would have been so easy to meet up with him and discuss our time together on the squadron, and we might even have been writing these memoirs together. But at least I have been in contact with his son and one of his daughters. They were amazed at me turning up and being able to tell them things about Geoff's past that they did not know. It seems that he talked very little about his wartime experiences flying Beaufighters over Burma. This was an added incentive for me, as I feel I am writing these memoirs for two families, and also as a tribute to Geoff.

He was an officer and I was an NCO and as such we ate and drank in different messes and therefore did not socialise much together when off duty. However, when we were in the air, rank was forgotten. We had a good working relationship and he would frequently consult me when we had to make decisions. Geoff was a good pilot. He was courageous but not a daredevil and did not take unnecessary risks. I think he always remembered that there was somebody else aboard in the back seat! Apart from surviving the ever-present hazards of the weather (especially during the monsoon period), enemy opposition and the risk of engine failure, I owe the fact that I am alive and writing this today to Geoff's skill and endurance in coping with so many hours of hazardous low flying.

The Author, plus friend, India 1944.

1.   Getting to Know the Beaufighter

After the excitement, and indeed at times exhilaration, of eleven months spent training in Canada, returning to wartime Britain was like coming down to earth with a bump.

First there was the food. I had grown used to being asked whether I wanted one egg or two with my bacon and flapjacks for breakfast, and to having unlimited slices of white bread and 7lb tins of Canadian clover honey on every table. At other meals we had plentiful portions of steaks, chops, sausages, salmon, etc, and sweetcorn coming out of our ears. And if, at other times, one felt a bit peckish, there was always the NAAFI, where un-rationed chocolate, sweets, Dad's cookies and milkshakes of every flavour under the sun, could be had. It was depressing to be back again in the land of powdered egg, grey, unappetising utility bread, Spam, corned beef (if you were lucky), snoek, swede and where, in this Autumn of 1943, there was definitely *not* 'honey still for tea'. Also chocolate, sweets, soap, razor blades and many other little 'luxuries' were either rationed or hard to come by.

Then there was the weather. I had experienced virtually all the seasons in Canada, from Winter in Ontario, through the thaw and Spring on Prince Edward Island, to the near tropical Summer on Vancouver Island and had never had a day's illness. Although the winter in Ontario was severe, we had the right clothing for it and the living accommodation on all the stations where I trained was in properly constructed wooden barracks, well insulated and centrally heated. By contrast, the climate in England, even though it was still only September, was cold and damp. I caught several colds before the month was out.

But most depressing of all was that, not only had I left behind Betty, my Canadian girlfriend, but also I was now being split up from my NCO navigator pals with whom I had trained. Having completed an OTU, which had been orientated towards Coastal Command, on Hampden aircraft we had been posted to England as a crew of four. Geoff as Pilot, me as Navigator and two Canadian Air Gunners, one of whom was also a Wireless Operator. Some Hampdens were still being used on Coastal Command work but we were told that they were being phased out and no more crews were required. Also, in my case, I was told that as a Navigator/W I was too valuable to be used on aircraft which also had another Wireless Operator, and would have to do my operational flying on aircraft intended for a two man crew, such as the Beaufighter or Mosquito.

The two Canadian lads were sent to Bomber Command, Geoff was sent to a Beaufighter conversion unit and I was sent to No.3 School of General Reconnaissance at Squires Gate, notwithstanding the fact that I had already done a similar course in Canada. I spent the month of October at Squires Gate and maybe this was a blessing in disguise, because at the end of this time I was posted to RAF Catfoss where I met up with Geoff. When we had first been split up he had asked for me to be re-united with him as his Navigator, but I had been doubtful whether this would happen and was pleased to find that it had. However we found that we were not supposed to be at Catfoss and we spent a week in limbo there while the ponderous RAF administration discovered that we should be at No.9 OTU at Crosby-on-Eden near Carlisle. We eventually arrived there on the 3rd of November.

As I have indicated, my morale was low since returning to England. Now it got lower. Crosby-on-Eden was a dump and so began the most miserable winter of my wartime service with the RAF, culminating with the crash in the following February.

It was here at Crosby that I first experienced the arctic conditions of living in a Nissen hut in wintertime. The bare concrete floor and uninsulated corrugated iron roof made them damp cold and draughty, to an extent scarcely alleviated by the pathetic coke stoves which were supposed to heat them. Because I had arrived late I was put in a hut, some distance from the Mess and a bit off the beaten track, which was occupied by only two or three tradesmen NCO's who were seldom there, and only one flyer, who was on the permanent staff. He was a F/Sgt Smith who had the rather dicey job of flying a single engine Harvard aircraft towing a target drogue for trainee Beaufighter crews to practice air to air firing with live ammunition. He was a pleasant chap, and I liked him, but he had friends locally and spent a lot of time away from camp. Coupled with the fact that there were only five crews on our particular course, and the only ones I already knew were officers, I found it difficult to make new friends and I felt a bit isolated.

It was a problem what to do in the evenings to keep warm. The Mess tended to get rather rowdy and I was not much of a drinker at this time, but at least there was a room for reading and writing letters. The only good thing about this camp was the cinema because they changed the programme about three times a week. Nevertheless it was not surprising that about half the personnel on the station fled to Carlisle every evening on the first of several RAF buses that left at about five o'clock, even though it sometimes meant forgoing their evening meal. I seldom went into the town myself as its pubs, clubs and bars did not appeal to me.

The training course itself was completely different to the OTU in Canada and seemed to be somewhat disjointed. The unit had a miscellany of ageing Beaufighters and was split into three Flights, each of which we were attached to in turn to carry out different types of exercises. With No.2 Flight we did some formation flying locally, and some night take-offs and landings. With No.3 Flight it was again mostly local flying practising air to air and air to ground firing. The aircraft on this Flight were fitted with cine camera guns which were used for simulated attacks on other Beaufighters, and we also used live ammunition to fire at target drogues towed by the Harvard flown by F/Sgt Smith. The live firing exercises were carried out over a designated area of water in the Solway Firth. Because this was going on in December and January the winter weather often prevented us from completing the exercises because of low cloud and poor visibility.

I did not like this preoccupation with air combat because for several weeks I was hardly doing any navigation or wireless operating, but was just acting as Observer, giving Geoff instructions for taking evasive action when 'enemy' aircraft attacked from the rear. I realised that this was yet another onerous task, and a vital one, that a Navigator/W would have to do in a two man aircraft such as the Beaufighter.

The aircraft on No.4 Flight were adapted to carry a relatively new weapon, Rocket Projectiles, and we were to get instruction on these and to carry out several firing exercises on a firing range which was only a few minutes flying away. Also, with this flight, we were to do several operational flying exercises of four to five hours duration.

However there was a hiatus at this point in the course since No.4 Flight were not ready to take us and so one weekend, towards the end of January, we were given 72 hour leave passes. I did not have anywhere to go, or rather no real pals to go with, and it was a measure of my despondency at the time that I decided to go home to Greenford, even though it would mean that effectively I would only have one day. I thought that if I could sleep in a warm place for a change and have a bath instead of showers in the chilly ablutions room I would feel better, and the change might recharge my batteries as they say. The leave started at noon on Friday and the journey down to London, in a crowded train, seemed to go on for ever. By the time I got the Underground train and arrived at Ealing Broadway station it had just turned ten o'clock.

With several other passengers I emerged from the dimly lit foyer and groped my way in the blackout across the road to the bus stop at the corner of Haven Green where we joined the bus queue. At that moment the air raid sirens went. I had not heard that chilling wail since I had left England a year previously.

"That's all I need!" said a voice behind me. I turned round and saw a young girl, in her late teens, who went on to say "There hasn't been an alert here for several weeks and it *would* have to be *tonight*. I should have been home over an hour ago and my parents will be worried sick." At that moment an Air Raid Warden appeared and directed us to the nearest air raid shelter. Most of the people left, leaving me, the girl and two others anxiously waiting for the bus. Out of the darkness appeared, most unexpectedly, a Bus Inspector. He suggested that, rather than stand out in the open, we should go back into the station foyer and he would come and tell us when the bus came. This we did, and, as we entered through the blackout doors into the lit foyer, I saw how very pretty the girl was. She was greeted by a few wolf whistles and catcalls from a small group of Squaddies who were sitting on the floor in the far corner, engaged in rowdy conversation. She looked round nervously and, perhaps because she saw that I was a sergeant, she stayed by my side and said, "May I pretend that I am with you?" There were no seats and so we sat on the floor, against the wall and talked.

Her name was Clare, she was 19, an only child and lived with her parents in Argyle Road, about a mile from where I lived at Greenford. She had a job in West London and had been to a dance that evening with some work colleagues but had stayed longer than she had meant to. Her parents were not on the phone and now that there was an Air Raid alert they would be very worried. She said that she simply must get home and there was no way she was going to spend the night in a public air raid shelter. I felt the same, for different reasons, but our hopes of getting the bus were dashed a few minutes later when the Inspector came back and said he was sorry but there would no more buses from Haven Green that night.

Clare remained silent for a few minutes and then said, "What are you going to do?" Since all seemed quiet outside, I had already decided that I would at least start walking and I told her so. "May I walk with you?" she said. I suppose I felt flattered that, after having talked to me for only about ten minutes, she felt able to trust me to walk home with her through the deserted, blacked-out suburban backstreets, and I would certainly like to have her company. I hesitated before replying, because if she came with me I would feel some responsibility for her and, as a member of the armed forces, I should not be encouraging such a young and vulnerable civilian to be out in the open during an air raid alert. However, since I felt that she was determined to attempt to walk anyway, I eventually said yes, provided that she agreed to wear my steel helmet which I was already starting to extricate from the straps that secured it to my gas mask haversack. She did not protest but simply said quietly "That's very nice of you, it will certainly make me feel a bit safer". I helped her put it on and shortened the chinstrap for her. We got up and went out into the darkness, giving rise to one or two ribald remarks from the Squaddies.

We both knew the route well, but knowing it from the inside of a bus is not the same as remembering every side street, kerb, lamppost and obstruction. We both had small torches with very restricted light but nevertheless we frequently clutched at one another as we stumbled along in the cold dark night. Clare talked about herself and how that in her latter teenage years she felt stifled by wartime restrictions. She did not have much of a social life and did not have a regular boyfriend. She felt that she should be doing more for the war effort and was considering volunteering for the ATS or WAAF, although she had not dared to discuss this with her parents as she knew that they would be very much against it.

Then, when I told her that less than two years previously I had been in a somewhat similar position and had left a reserved occupation to volunteer for the RAF as aircrew, she began plying me with questions. Had I regretted volunteering? If anyone had asked me that question earlier in the day I would have answered with a resounding 'Yes', but I found myself saying 'No', and proceeded to tell her about some of the more positive and exciting things that I had experienced. I told her how interesting it had been training as a wireless operator at Cranwell, where there were many young women – WAAFs – also training to be ground operators. I told her about crossing the Atlantic in a convoy, about learning air navigation, about crossing Canada by train and so on. I hardly mentioned Crosby-on-Eden. In just telling her these things I began to see my life in the RAF more in perspective.

As we walked on there were no sounds of any enemy activity nearby, although there were flashes and distant sounds of anti-aircraft gunfire coming from the direction of central London. Twice we were approached by Air Raid Wardens, emerging from their cubby-holes, who suggested that we should take cover but when they saw that I was a Sergeant, and that Clare was wearing a steel helmet, they did not bother overmuch.

We had been walking for just over an hour and were in Argyle Road, about quarter of a mile from Clare's house, when I heard a plane approaching from the north. It was not very high, probably around 4,000 feet, and the ominous sound of jinked engines, so familiar during the Blitz, left me in no doubt that it was German. I started to look round for a doorway or somewhere to take cover when suddenly our unprotected ears were assaulted by a deafening succession of violent bangs as the guns of a nearby anti-aircraft battery opened up. This meant that we were in imminent danger from falling shrapnel, and we had to do something quickly. I noticed a side-street on our left, where I saw that there was an end of terrace house which had a plain brick wall right down to the pavement. I hurriedly led Clare towards it and explained to her that if we stood close up against the wall we would be largely shielded from falling shrapnel by the building, as the plane and the bursting shells, although above, were behind us. There was, of course, some risk of these wickedly jagged bits of metal ricocheting off the roofs opposite, but she probably knew this. We huddled together against the wall and in moments between the firing of the guns and the bursting of shells overhead we heard the clatter of shrapnel on surrounding roofs, and of bits of tiles falling in the road. It was rather frightening. I felt Clare shiver and put my arm round her. She held her gloved hands over her ears and turned her face into the lapel of my greatcoat, perhaps fearful of injury to those lovely features.

Obviously the ack-ack battery did not do any serious damage to the plane because after a minute or two the firing stopped and I heard the plane droning away into the distance. All was quiet again and we resumed walking, our footsteps seeming to echo loudly in the cold, still night air after that appalling din. Clare was silent for a while then, as we got near to her house, she began to ask one or two 'fishing' questions, like 'do you have any plans for the weekend?' I think she had forgotten for the moment that I only had the one day, and I jokingly told her that I was going to sleep for 24 hours. When we got to her gate she invited me to come in for a cup of coffee and to meet her father, whom she said would want to thank me for walking her home. I declined the offer because I still had more than a mile to walk and I was so weary after the day's long journey and felt that if I once sat down I would never get started again. She gave me back my steel helmet and thanked me again.

"Well, at least you know where I live!" she laughed, as she walked up to her front door. But I never saw her again.

After walking on alone for about five minutes the All Clear sirens went, and I finally arrived home just before midnight. On the Saturday I really did sleep on until mid-afternoon, and did little else but bathe, eat and be warm. On the Sunday morning my father took me in the car to Ealing Broadway station and I set off on the long journey to Carlisle, only this time it did not seem nearly so long. I kept thinking about that walk through the dark with Clare, our conversation, and those few moments of shared space and time and real danger when she turned to me for protection. Clare will never know how much this brief encounter raised my morale. I was actually beginning to feel eager to get back and finish my training.

For the first few days back at Crosby we had some lectures and learned something about Rocket Projectiles. Compared with modern day weapons they were crude. They consisted of a steel tube about 2 inches in diameter by 40 inches long, with four fins welded at the back end and a warhead like an artillery shell fixed at the front. The tube was filled with cordite and the warhead with about 60lbs of high explosive. The tubes had lugs welded on so that they could be slid into the slots of guide rails which were fixed under the wings, four on each side, and they were retained by wire shear pins. Each tube had an igniter at the back end, which was plugged in to connections provided under the back edge of the wings, so that they could be fired electrically from the pilot's cockpit, either in pairs or the whole salvo of eight. When the cordite was ignited it burned rapidly like a rocket and the thrust sheared the retaining pin, allowing the projectile to shoot forward on a gravitational trajectory. When the cordite burned through it primed the warhead to explode on impact.

I remember that there was some discussion about what we should do in event of the cordite firing but the Rocket failing to leave the aircraft, or 'hanging up' as they called it. In this case the impact fuse would be primed. The short answer was that nothing could be done to get rid of it and the only advice, they said, was 'don't make a bumpy landing!' Nobody asked how safe the impact fuses were if the cordite had not been ignited, and I did not know then how relevant this would be to my own situation a couple of days later. Of course the whole plane had to be aimed at the target by the pilot using his reflector gunsight, and some practise was required in judging the correct height and distance from the target at which to fire. This was why we had to carry out live firing exercises on the range.

We started flying with No.4 Flight on the 4th of February. In the morning we did a descent through cloud exercise which involved me guiding Geoff back to the airfield by flying along a radio beam, and I was pleased to be using my skills as a wireless operator for the first time in several weeks. In the afternoon we switched to Beaufighter JL 774, which was one of those equipped for Rocket firing, and were flown to the range by a F/Lt Proctor, with Geoff standing behind him, for a demonstration attack. After landing we taxied to a point on the perimeter track where Geoff took over the aircraft whilst the armourers loaded eight more Rockets, which only took three or four minutes. It was common practice for this to be done with the engines still running because restarting hot engines often caused problems and would waste time. Fitting the Rockets to the rails was done under the wing from the back so the armourers were well clear of the propellers. A disadvantage of this procedure was that whilst the engines were idling the cylinder head temperatures would gradually creep up and there was an upper limit, specified in the pilots manual, above which it would not be safe to take-off.

However all was well and we took off, flew to the range and made our first rocket attack. Although the 'score' would later be assessed by the party manning the range, Geoff new he had done well. We landed at about 1625 hours and taxied to the re-loading point for the second trip which we were scheduled to make. On the way we had a message from the Control Tower asking us to postpone our second trip until the next morning because it was too near the deadline for cessation of flying, and manning of the range. When there were no night flying exercises planned the flarepath was not lit and the Crash Tender and groundstaff crews went off duty just after sunset, which was at about 1700 hours on this February afternoon.

The round trip to the range only took about 35 minutes and Geoff protested that there was still time, and also pointed out that we were detailed for an early morning take-off on an operational flying exercise the following morning. The Controller then agreed that we could do another trip and telephoned the range staff instructing them to stay at their posts. I heard later that they had been all packed up and about to get into their truck to dash back to camp, perhaps for the evening exodus to Carlisle, and they cannot have been too pleased.

We reached the loading point only to find that the armourers, normally so adept at speedy re-arming, had not been expecting us to take-off again and took longer than usual. To make matters worse one Rocket would not fit into its rail properly, and it had to be changed. Meanwhile we were sitting there, engines idling, cylinder head temperatures rising, and Geoff getting more and more impatient as he made frantic signs to the armourers to get a move on.   We had two calls from the Controller asking what the delay was. The second call was an ultimatum that if we did not take-off within the next five minutes we would not be allowed to go. At almost the last possible minute we got the thumbs up from the armourers and taxied out. As Geoff lined up on the runway he observed that the cylinder head temperatures were noticeably higher than for the last take-off, but still within the limit. He opened the throttles and, with the familiar roar and surge of power from the two 1600 brake horsepower Hercules engines we quickly gathered speed. We had just got airborne, I remember seeing him operate the lever which began to raise the undercarriage, when I glimpsed something out of the corner of my eye that made me turn and look out of my Cupola. From under the port wing I saw some smoke coming from the exhaust of the port engine. I said over the intercom, "There's black smoke coming from…" , but before I had finished the aircraft had reared up into a steep climb and bank to the left.

This was one of those moments when time seemed to slip into bottom gear, and events were experienced a millisecond at a time. At first I actually felt anger because I thought that Geoff was putting our lives at risk by trying to do some spectacular take-off manoeuvre. Common sense told me that the Beaufighter was in an attitude that could not possibly be sustained without stalling. In spite of the fact that I had seen the smoke coming from the port engine it was several more fractions of a second before I realised what was happening. It was every pilot's nightmare. The port engine had cut out completely whilst the starboard engine was still at full throttle and we had barely reached flying speed.

Somehow Geoff managed to get the aircraft on to an even keel before we slammed back on to the ground with such force that I felt it must surely break up. It didn't. Before the impact he had reversed the undercarriage lever, abandoning any thought of trying to take-off, thinking that he might attempt to land on the rest of the runway. But instead we bounced high into the air and before we crashed down again he saw that we had swung right off the runway and were heading across the grass towards the edge of the airfield where there was a large maintenance hanger. Judging that we would not be able to stop in time he started raising the undercarriage again and cut the starboard engine before the next sickening crash into the ground. To me this second impact seemed worse and I think I momentarily blacked out. I don't know whether the undercarriage was fully up at the moment we hit the ground but it would probably have given way completely anyway.

We careered on with a series of bounces of lessening magnitude, each followed by sickening thuds and alarming crunching sounds from underneath, during which time I was violently jolted about, until the Beaufighter finally skidded to a halt on its belly. Almost before it had stopped I flipped open the two toggles which unlocked my cupola, flung it open, even remembered to pull the plug of my intercom lead out of its socket, and jumped the six feet or so to the ground. With an overwhelming sense of relief that I was safe and standing on the good earth I pushed back my flying helmet and was engulfed in silence, so wonderful after the din of the past few minutes.

But was I safe and was all silent? There was a sizzling sound coming from under the plane which galvanized my brain back into action. This was a moment of great potential danger, such as I had seen on films – a crashed plane coming to rest apparently largely in one piece then, after a few seconds, being engulfed in a fire ball. All it needed was petrol from a fractured fuel pipe or a ruptured fuel tank seeping along the ground and coming into contact with the hot exhaust pipes. Other thoughts raced through my head. What about the rockets, the cordite in the tubes, the high explosive heads with impact fuses?

The drill is for each aircrew member to get out of the plane as quickly as possible and run to at least 50 yards away to be out of danger, but where was Geoff? I looked forward and saw that he was still in his cockpit and was not getting out. Had he been knocked unconscious? What should I do? Seemingly impelled by the will of my deeper consciousness I took a couple of steps forward and climbed up on to the wing where I stood beside his cockpit. But in the fraction of a second that it took to do this I was also aware of a myriad of thoughts racing through my brain such as – 'run!, it will be madness to step on the wing, you'll be standing over one of the petrol tanks, what about the Rockets underneath and the magazines of 20 mm cannon shells in the fuselage beside you, the whole lot could explode at any minute, I don't want to die!, if Geoff is unconscious you won't be able to lift him out unaided, the crash crew will be here any minute with someone in an asbestos suit, it is their job to get him out, run!' – But my deeper consciousness, which had witnessed these thoughts, had ignored them.

Geoff was not unconscious but was somewhat dazed. He still had his flying helmet on, with its built-in earphones, and was holding his microphone over his mouth with his right hand, whilst fumbling with the handle of his sliding cockpit canopy, which was half open, with his left. I heard him speaking into the microphone saying, "Denny, are you all right?"

"Yes", I shouted, "get out quick!" But he could not hear me because his earphones were not working.

Meanwhile I got hold of the exterior handle of his canopy and pulled it fully open. This meant that it was pulled right out of his hand but he still did not realise that I was standing outside the fuselage right beside him. Again he said into the microphone, "Denny, are you all right?"

Again I shouted, even louder, *"Get out quick!"* and this time I tapped him on the shoulder. With a great start he saw me and clambered out of the cockpit. Together we jumped off the wing and ran to a safe distance.

We were congratulating ourselves on having escaped without injury, and indeed we were actually laughing about the incident at the cockpit, which now seemed so ridiculous, when the crash tender arrived about half a minute later. The crew were relieved to see that we were safe and called to us to stay where we were whilst they proceeded to spray foam on the engines as a precaution. I do not think that there had been any leakage of petrol, and the alarming sizzling sound that I had heard had probably been due to the hot exhaust pipes being in contact with the damp grass.

At this point a second vehicle, a rather ancient-looking military ambulance, arrived and stopped a bit further away and behind the aircraft where we were standing. The driver, probably also a medical orderly, did not get out as he would have seen that we were apparently unhurt. The other occupant was a medical officer, who got out and started to walk towards us. Geoff and I stopped talking in open mouthed surprise as we saw that this medical officer was not a man but an attractive young woman WAAF Section Officer. Furthermore, she was smartly dressed in her blue barathea uniform, that is tunic and skirt, as opposed to blue battledress, which all personnel normally wore when on duty. What an incongruous sight it was as she walked towards us, delicately stepping over the trail of debris and churned up muddy earth left by our Beaufighter! It had been my understanding that whenever flying was in progress there had to be on call an MO who was qualified as a surgeon, and this young woman, who could not have been much older than me, could surely not have had the necessary experience? (I did hear it rumoured that the MO who had been on call that afternoon had slipped off into town early and left her to cover for him. If this were true it would have been in keeping with the whole ethos of the place as I perceived it.)

Whatever the Section Officer had been doing at the time it must have been quite a shock for her to get an emergency call to attend the site of a crashed aircraft on the other side of the airfield, not knowing what situation or injuries she might have to cope with. As she reached us she was rather nervous, but obviously showing signs of great relief that we were apparently uninjured. She questioned us as to whether we felt any ill effects and suggested that we go back with her to the sick quarters for a check-up. I remember she mentioned the possibility of shock but this did not mean much to me at the time. However we both protested that this was unnecessary as, apart from bruises, we felt all right. In retrospect I think that she should have been more insistent as, after all, we were still high on adrenaline! However, before she left, she did make us promise to go and see her if either of us felt any delayed effects.

By this time the aircraft had been declared safe and we returned to it to collect our parachutes. It was badly damaged and was obviously a write-off. More ground staff arrived and began to survey the damage and to see how they could best retrieve the rockets. It was only then we noticed that two of the rockets had been ripped off the underside and were lying on the grass some distance away. Obviously, provided that the cordite had not been ignited, the impact fuses in the warheads were safer than I thought. I wished I had known that earlier!

Eventually, a jeep came to take us back to our respective living quarters. I felt elated. I had been in a crash and had walked away from it virtually unharmed. Before going to the Mess I walked to the guardroom to book an early call for 0530 hours the following morning and so I arrived in the dining hall quite late. The dining hall at Crosby had long refectory-type tables and was the first NCOs' Mess I had been in where WAAFs served at the tables instead of the cafeteria service I had been used to in Canada. Most of the tables had already been cleared, leaving two at the end for latecomers like myself. I sat down and was brought my meal but, as others left, I was alone at one end of the table.

Although it was warm in the hall I still felt cold and shivered once or twice. Half way through my meal I was alarmed to find that I was having difficulty holding my knife and fork because my hands were trembling. At the other end of the table three WAAFs were chatting away as they began to clear this last table. One of them brought me my tea which was in a china mug but, although I was desperate for a hot drink, I found that I could not lift it with one hand without it wobbling so much that some tea spilt on the table. Although the WAAFs were not paying any particular attention to me they were quite close and occasionally one would look in my direction, I suppose to see whether I had finished. I felt very embarrassed in case they saw me. In the end I had to hold the mug in both hands and slouch low over the table to gulp down tea surreptitiously when none of them was looking my way. I was feeling light-headed and it slowly dawned on me that I was suffering from shock. Maybe that WAAF Medical Officer was not as young and inexperienced as I had thought, and I should have taken her advice.

I left the Mess and wandered back to my Nissen hut. Nobody else was there, the stove was out and it was very cold. It was now about eight o'clock and I decided that the best thing was to get into bed. Even with three blankets and my greatcoat over me I still did not feel warm but before I got to sleep F/Sgt Smith came and was surprised to find me in bed so early. He said that Geoff had been on the phone with a message to say that we were both to report to the Chief Flying Instructors office at 1130 hours next morning, but that our early flight was still on as planned. We would be back in time for the interview. Even as he relayed the message, its purport seemed to suddenly dawn on him. "That crash", he said. "It was *you* wasn't it? Are you all right?" I told him that I was, but he must have thought that I looked a bit shaky, because he began to show almost paternal concern. Did I want a hot drink? Should he phone the MO? He even managed to find me another blanket. Finally, I persuaded him that I would be all right in the morning and he went back to the Mess, promising that he would be quiet when he came back in so as not to wake me.

At 0530 hours the next morning I was wakened from a deep sleep by an Airman, fumbling with his torch and a little notebook, in which I had to sign for my morning call. After he went, I lay in bed for a moment with a terrible sinking feeling as I remembered where I was, the events of the previous evening and what I had to do. No way, I thought, was I going to get into a Beaufighter and take-off again. I decided that I would get dressed and meet Geoff in the Briefing Room and tell him that I was unfit to fly and that I would report sick later. Sick? Slowly I realised that the peculiar 'spaced out' feeling of the previous evening was gone. The shock I had suffered from must have only been mild and, apart from some tender bruises, there was nothing wrong with me now. I was just scared at the thought of flying again. But at that moment thoughts of Clare, and our conversation, came in to my head. I recalled how she had somehow re-kindled the feelings of patriotism and duty that had led me to volunteer to join the RAF in the first place. After all, I had always known that there would be dangers in flying and now that I had qualified as a Navigator it was my job to fly, and fly I must.

The best thing about getting up and performing one's ablutions in the freezing cold conditions at Crosby on a February morning was that when you finally got dressed in a thick aircrew polo-neck sweater, serge battle dress, fur-lined flying boots and Mae West, you actually started to feel warm.

Thus it was that, after a quick cup of tea, I collected my navigation bag and parachute and made my way to the Briefing Room. There were four crews detailed to fly this morning and I saw that we were included in the list of names and aircraft numbers chalked up on the board. Somehow, I had expected to find our trip cancelled.

After a few minutes Geoff came in. His first concern was to ask if I was all right and how did I feel about going up again? I simply told him that I was OK, having decided not to tell him about the after-effects I had experienced the previous evening. He then confided in me that he thought it was implicit in the message that he had received indirectly from the Chief Flying Instructor, who had been off the camp at the time, that we should not fly again until after the interview, but as he had received no specific instructions, and it appeared that nobody had even bothered to check up that we were detailed to fly early this very morning, he felt that he just wanted to get into the air again as quickly as possible. If it was OK with me, he said, then we should just go.

These operational flying exercises were usually along set routes and we got details of ours, OFE.2, from the Briefing Officer. We were to go westwards to Rathlin Island, off the coast of Northern Ireland, and then northwards up among the Western Isles to Eigg and then on to Stornaway and back. The round trip would take about three and a half hours. The Meteorological Officer then gave us estimates of winds and weather conditions, which were far from good. Further north there would be a lot of rain, low cloud and poor visibility. I filled in my flight plan and then we were taken out to the aircraft.

Ours was a Mk.VI Beaufighter, No.5154, which we then boarded. Whilst I checked the intercom and my WT transmitter and receiver, Geoff did his routine cockpit check. The engines were started, run up and checked. I am sure that Geoff did all this more thoroughly than ever before. He must have been satisfied that all was well because he then gave the ground crew the thumbs up, whereupon the wheel chocks were removed and we taxied out to the runway. During this time I had nothing to do and I felt nervous tension mounting.

We received permission to take-off and Geoff lined up on the runway. "O.K. for take-off?" he said, as he always did just before opening the throttles. This was partly a final check that we were in communication through the intercom and to make sure that I could not see any reason why we should not. The next thirty seconds or so was going to be quite an ordeal and I felt like replying, "No, stop, I don't want to go!" but my mouth said, "Yes, O.K."

He pushed the throttle levers forward and once more I heard the roar of those Hercules engines and felt that surge of power as we gathered speed. It was not so bad for Geoff, as he was fully occupied. Some of these older Beaufighters had a tendency to swing when full take-off power was applied and for the first few seconds great concentration was required just to keep it straight. In addition to this, he would obviously be monitoring all the instruments even more carefully than usual for the first signs of anything amiss. But I had nothing to do except to note the time of take-off. I felt us lift off. I felt the undercarriage come up and heard it lock. I felt the flaps come up and I felt Geoff ease the throttles back from take-off power to a normal climb. It was a normal take-off such as I had experienced many times before.

"Well, that one was all right!" said Geoff cheerfully. "What's the first course?" I gave him the course to steer for Rathlin Island and we were on our way. From then on I had plenty to do. We were soon in and out of cloud but I did get a pinpoint as we crossed the Ayrshire coast, a few miles south of Girvan, which enabled me to check our track made good and groundspeed. I calculated a more accurate wind velocity and made a slight alteration to the course. Also I managed to send my first routine wireless message to base, which we were required to do every thirty minutes or so. We arrived over Rathlin Island, which I spotted through a gap in the clouds after about 35 minutes, and then turned on to a northerly course, heading for the island of Islay.

After a few minutes flying, the weather ahead rapidly got worse, making even the Met Officer's gloomy report seem to have been optimistic. Low cloud and mist made it too dangerous to try and get down to sea level. This exercise was supposed to be like a reconnaissance trip, up among the Western Isles to Stornoway, observing any shipping, etc, but after flying on in cloud for about 15 minutes Geoff decided that it was pointless going on and asked for a course back to base. I calculated a course, from a DR position in cloud, which would take us directly back across Kirkcudbrightshire. I sent another wireless message to base, telling them that we were returning due to bad weather. All this was, of course, routine stuff for a Navigator/Wireless Operator, but I was feeling pleased that I was carrying out my duties in a normal manner. Yesterday afternoon's crash, and the feelings of apprehension before taking off again were all in the past. As we got near the Solway Firth the cloud began to break up a bit and I was able to check that we were on track. We landed safely, after having been airborne for only one and a half hours, but long enough to know that we had both regained our confidence.

After dumping our flying kit we met at the Chief Flying Instructor's office at 1130 hours as instructed. Geoff had said earlier that he was worried about this interview because he thought they would blame him for the crash, saying that he must have taken off with overheated engines. He went in first and told me afterwards that he had been given a mild rebuke for having flown again prior to the interview, but the CFI could not make much of this since it was due to lack of communication among his own staff that Geoff had not been given any specific instruction about this. However he came out smiling, saying that they had already found the cause of the engine failure and he was not to blame.

It transpired that the engine was fitted with non-standard ignition plugs, having a smaller spark gap than normal. This did not greatly affect the performance except that they would obviously tend to 'carbon up' more readily under adverse conditions. The maximum permitted cylinder head temperature for take-off with these plugs was nearly 50 degrees C lower than normal. This fact may have been recorded somewhere in the aircraft's maintenance log book but, incredibly, a note had not been brought forward from day to day on the Daily Inspection sheets which had to be noted and signed by the Pilot before taking the plane up. Nor had this vital piece of information been communicated verbally, and neither was there any warning notice on the instrument panel in the aircraft cockpit. For normal take-offs there was still plenty of margin, but this was one of No.4 Flight's aircraft, frequently being used for short flights to the Rocket Range, and the ground staff were well aware that the practice of re-loading, with engines idling, might lead to engines being hotter than usual. Under these circumstances it was a serious oversight for the revised temperature limit not to have been brought to the attention of the pilot, an oversight that led to a Beaufighter being written off and could easily have led to Geoff and I being killed.

I also had an interview with the CFI but this was just a formality. He asked me how I felt and I assured him that, now that I had been on this morning's trip I knew that I would be all right. Unexpectedly, he asked me if I was happy flying with Geoff, to which I replied that I was, and that I had every confidence in him as my pilot. As I left he actually used those words, which have become such a cliché that I hardly like to quote them, 'Good show, Spencer!'

For the next eleven days we put in a lot of flying hours. We did three more trips to the Rocket firing range and six more navigation exercises, one of them wholly at night. There were no more dramatic incidents except that late one afternoon the weather over the Irish Sea clamped down and we had the experience of making a precautionary landing, in the dark, at a fully operational RAF airfield at Valley, on the Isle of Anglesey, where we stayed overnight.

We completed the course and were posted from No.9 OTU, as a qualified Beaufighter crew, on the 18th of February 1944. From my point of view this ended the dreariest four months of my time in the RAF and I was glad to leave Crosby-on-Eden. The assessment slip they put in my Log Book graded me as 'average' both as Navigator and Wireless Operator. If I had had to give an assessment of the Wing Commander then in charge it would have read something like:-

'Below Average. You need to eradicate the nine 'til five attitude of some of your staff to their job. You need to instil more enthusiasm into them and to improve communication between them. More diligence is required by maintenance staff whose oversight led to a Beaufighter being written off, and could have led to the crew being killed. Pull your socks up, there's a war on!'

Maybe that was it, they were war weary.

2.   The 7,000 Mile Journey Part I ~ Across the Bay of Biscay

Life is unpredictable, never more so than in wartime. Because our operational training on Beaufighters at No.9 OTU had included the use of Rocket Projectiles, a comparatively new weapon currently being used mainly against enemy shipping, Geoff and I had assumed that we would be posted to an operational squadron of Coastal Command in the U.K. We were therefore surprised to hear, just before leaving Crosby-on-Eden on 16th February, that we were being sent overseas to the Far East, to what was then called India Air Command. Not only that but to get there we were to be used as a ferry crew to fly a brand new Beaufighter all the way from the U.K. to Allahabad in India, a total journey of around 7,000 miles.

We were given seven days 'embarkation' leave and I went home to Greenford. I found that my friend Eric, who lived next door, was also on leave. He had just completed his training as a Flight Engineer at RAF St. Athan, where he was due to return on the coming Sunday. St. Athan was close to where his aunt was living at Barry Island and he suggested that we both went there for a long weekend. On the spur of the moment I decided to go and it proved to be a pleasant interlude after the dreariness of Crosby-on-Eden.

Barry Island had a small beach, still accessible to the public, and a seaside funfair, which made it seem like a little haven of pre-war England, or in this case Wales. I met Eric's pretty sixteen-year-old cousin Jill and we all spent a carefree Saturday fooling about on the beach and at the funfair. Jill seemed thrilled to have not one but two aircrew sergeants escorting her around!

I spent the remaining few days at home on a bit of a high after my encounter with Jill. On the 21st February I had to go into London to the Wellcome Research Institution to get immunised against Yellow Fever. Maybe it was the jab of the needle that brought me down to earth with the realisation that the day after next I had to report to No.304 FTU at Melton Mowbray. Then it would be off overseas for goodness knows how long to goodness knows where, but certainly nowhere very pleasant if I needed to be protected against something as dreadful as Yellow Fever!

Melton Mowbray was a ferry and transport unit where new aircraft were flown in direct from the manufacturers' works, sometimes by women ferry pilots of the Air Transport Auxiliary (ATA). Here they were checked and any special items of RAF equipment added before they were flown off to squadrons or wherever they were needed. Because, in the case of our Beaufighter, the first stage of our journey would be a long flight over the sea to North Africa we were told that we would have to make a fuel consumption test flight as soon as it arrived.

Meanwhile we were issued with tropical clothing and had to hand in some surplus items which they said we would not be needing. Sadly, I said goodbye to my greatcoat, which had seen me through a Canadian winter and, more recently, the rigours of three winter months at cold, damp Crosby-on-Eden. The only winter clothing I retained was my blue battledress, my white Guernsey polo-neck aircrew sweater and my fur-lined flying boots.

We had lectures on health and hygiene in tropical countries, survival in the jungle and suchlike. There were visits to the medical quarters at intervals for several other inoculations, the worst being for Typhus. This involved two injections, spaced apart so that the second was to be given within four days before leaving the country.

Geoff's pal Steve and his navigator Sammy, who had been with us at Crosby, had been allocated the first Beaufighter and had already gone, but our aircraft was not delivered on the day promised, so we spent several days waiting about. Eventually it arrived on 3rd March.

It was Beaufighter NE.534, which I believe came from the shadow factory at Old Mixon and not from Bristol's main works at Filton. For the consumption test the fuel level in the tanks had to be actually checked by dipstick before take-off and then again on landing. By the time it was made ready it was 1515 hours before we took off on our test flight. We simply had to fly, straight and level, for a minimum of three hours at the designated economical cruising speed of 180 knots. Being wartime, we couldn't just fly anywhere, but were restricted to flying back and forth within a fairly narrow air corridor in a southwest direction to the Bristol Channel. Strangely, this took us very close to Barry Island, but I did not get a good look at it because visibility was poor. It was nothing like that bright, sunny Saturday I had spent there two weeks previously. Indeed, as we finally headed back to Melton Mowbray the weather over Leicestershire worsened and it became very hazy.

About ten minutes before ETA I had a moment of panic because visibility was so poor that I couldn't see where we were, and it would soon be dark. But, luckily, after a couple of minutes, I spotted a group of large radio masts below us, which I recognised as the old international broadcasting station at Hillmorton. Making a slight alteration to our course we found the airfield at Melton Mowbray, where Geoff made a good landing, almost in twilight, at 1820 hours.

Next morning we were told that the calculated fuel consumption was within the prescribed limits. However, they still had more things to do to make the aircraft ready. Some items of equipment and spares were stowed inside the fuselage, including a set of rocket rails, which were to be carried inside rather than fitted in position under the wings in order to reduce drag. The aircraft's cannons were loaded with drums of 20mm ammunition. We spent most of this day hanging about and expected that we would go the following morning.

However the next day we were summoned to the medical quarters and told that, in view of the time that had elapsed, the 'second' Typhus inoculation would have to be repeated and it was recommended that we should not fly until the following day. But when this came there was another problem. The weather had worsened, particularly down in Cornwall, where poor visibility and snowfalls had been reported. Since the first leg of our journey would be to RAF Portreath, where No.1 Overseas Aircraft Despatch Unit was located, our departure from Melton Mowbray was further postponed. Frustrating though this was, it proved to be a blessing in disguise, because during the day I felt quite ill. I had an adverse reaction to the last Typhus injection and spent most of that day lying on my bunk.

Finally, on the 7th of March, the meteorological report was better and we got clearance to go, but not until after mid-day. We took off at 1500 hours and set course for Portreath. For the first part of the journey the weather was bright, but with some scattered cumulus cloud and a fairly strong headwind. Again, by coincidence, our track took us over Barry Island and I was able to take a good look at it. I watched it as it slowly slipped away into the distance – and into the past.

On the other side of the Bristol Channel the sky became more overcast and we saw the first snow on the high ground of Exmoor. As we flew on across Devon into Cornwall it was obvious that the snowfall had been abnormally heavy for the time of year. The airfield at Portreath was on a plateau on a high cliff, adjacent to a tiny bay and fishing village. I had known from my map that it was situated near the coastline but as Geoff did a circuit prior to landing I realised that, in fact, one edge of the airfield *was* the coastline. The main runway, which had been cleared of snow and on which we were about to land, ended only yards from the cliff edge, with a drop of about 300 feet to the rocks below. It was not a runway you could afford to overshoot!

Because of the headwinds, the flight had taken longer than we had anticipated and it was 1645 hours before Geoff made his landing. For the second time within a few days he was having to touch down on an unfamiliar runway in rapidly fading light, a condition which most pilots dislike, but he made a good job of it. As we taxied to a dispersal point I realised that I was feeling rather groggy again with the after-effects of that inoculation. I just wanted to have a meal, find a bed and get some sleep, so that hopefully I would feel fit for the long flight next day. But it was not to be. We had no sooner clambered out of the aircraft when a truck came and whisked us away into the darkness, driving at quite a speed along winding country lanes which had snow banked up high at the edges. The driver said he had been instructed to take us straight to the 'Evening Briefing' and we had to get there by 1715 hours. I gathered that this briefing was essential for all crews who would be departing the next day. The room was large but mercifully warm compared with the bitter cold outside but I felt feverish and found it difficult to concentrate.

As they talked I began to realise that for the first part of the journey across the Bay of Biscay we would be virtually 'running the gauntlet' across what was a veritable aerial and naval 'no man's land' where anything could happen and frequently did. We would be crossing the routes of U-boats, which might be surfaced on the sea, and large, long-range Dornier 177 aircraft, both on their journeys to and from the Atlantic, where they preyed on Allied shipping convoys.

In the sea area which we would be traversing, both U-boats and Dorniers were sometimes escorted by formations of Junkers 88's, which wouldn't hesitate to attack a lone Beaufighter. Indeed, we heard that only a few days previously a formation of Beaufighters from No.248 Squadron, which had just moved to Portreath from Predannack, had gone to investigate a sighting of a crippled U-boat. They had found it to be escorted by as many as ten Ju.88s and an aerial combat ensued, with losses on both sides.

Another menace was that the Luftwaffe, hard pressed though they were to provide aircraft elsewhere, had recently made available a small number of Focke-Wulf 190 fighters to operate from coastal bases in Brittany. To us, the Fw.190 was deadly. It had a maximum speed almost twice that of a Beaufighter, was highly manoeuvrable and heavily armed. Not only did it have four 20mm cannons and two machine guns but some were said to have a 30mm cannon mounted to fire through the propeller boss. A single Beaufighter would not stand a chance against one. However, its range limited it to an effective radius of action of about 230 miles from the French coast.

I gathered that No.1 OADU were now despatching an increasing number of aircraft, several a day, to North Africa.

These were mostly heavily-laden transport planes. The most vulnerable ones, particularly if they were carrying military VIP passengers, sometimes had long-range fighter escorts of Beaufighters or Mosquitos for part of the way across the bay. But there would be no such protection for us! As an armed operational warplane simply being ferried from one country to another, we would be flying alone. Our only tactic would be to fly initially southwest from Lands End, heading towards the open Atlantic, which would take us out of range at least of single-engined fighters as quickly as possible. How far we could go before turning southwards, to make a landfall off the coast of Spain, would be up to me to calculate. Our destination was an airfield near Rabat, a town about 60 miles north of Casablanca in Morocco.

I was given a Mercator chart covering the whole coastal sea area down to North Africa, a map of Morocco and some W/T information on call signs and frequencies. Our brief was that we must plan the flight so that we would have sufficient fuel left to give us a margin of between thirty and forty-five minutes flying time on arrival. Geoff reckoned that our maximum duration would be six hours forty-five minutes. Accordingly, I drew up a flight plan, based on forecast winds, which would allow us to reach a point 250 miles from the French coast before turning south, but which would give an overall flight time of not more than six hours ten minutes. We were to leave just after sunrise the next morning.

We were instructed to maintain W/T silence except in an emergency, or to report the position of a U-boat if we saw one. Also, for the latter part of the journey down the coast of Portugal, we were warned that we must stay strictly outside the limit of their territorial waters. Portugal was, of course, a neutral country, but I well remember being surprised at what one of the briefing officers told us. With an air of one who considered himself to be a bit of a wag, he said, "If you are thinking of having engine trouble as you pass Lisbon and making a precautionary landing there, forget it! Your aircraft will be impounded and you will be interned. True, the internment camps are more like holiday camps and you may even have freedom of movement into the town on occasions.

You might think that you've struck it lucky for the rest of the war, but you'd be wrong. Within a couple of weeks some civilian clothes, identity papers, a railway warrant and a little money will mysteriously appear on your bed. You will be directed to the railway station to take a train down south, into Spain and thence to Gibraltar. You will be back in England within a few days, facing a Court of Inquiry, and with the Air Ministry wanting to know what you have done with their brand new aircraft."

I was in that briefing room for nearly two hours, but it was only when I came out and the cold air hit me that I realised just how bad I felt. I had a slight sore throat and was aching all over. I was dropped off at a large Mess hall where, although I was not hungry, I stayed for some while, mainly because it was warm. After that, I had to walk some distance, again in the freezing night air. I silently cursed the equipment storekeeper at Melton Mowbray who had persuaded me to hand in my greatcoat, particularly when I found out that the only available accommodation was in an unheated Nissen hut. There was nothing to do but get into bed and pile blankets on top of me. I spent a very restless night, feverishly hot one minute and freezing cold the next. It reminded me of the night after the crash at Crosby-on-Eden, only a month ago, when I was suffering from shock. Only this time I was suffering from – well a touch of Typhus, I guess!

My early morning call at five came all too soon. I must have got up, got ready and had breakfast like a Zombie, because I remember none of it. The first recollection I have is of walking to the agreed pick-up point with one question dominating my mind. Was I well enough to fly? The sun had not long risen and was shining on heaps of snow that lay piled up all around. It was a bright and breezy March morning and, truth to tell, I was beginning to feel a bit better, except that the arm where I had been inoculated was very sore. Geoff had not had any after effects from that last inoculation and I had not told him how bad I had felt again the previous afternoon. Only when I met up with him, and he casually asked me how I was, did I make my decision to go. I simply told him that I was alright, but did mention my painful arm.

We were driven out to the aircraft which had been re-fuelled, inspected and de-iced. The ground crew were standing by with the mobile starting accumulators in position and they had opened the entrance hatches under the fuselage all ready for us. I stood by the fuselage and gingerly put on my Mae West and parachute harness, being careful not to hurt my arm, but when I came to get on board I realised that I could not do it. You needed to use both arms to hoist yourself up through the hatch and I had to get one of the ground crew to help me get aboard. Doubts entered my mind again as to whether I really ought to be going. But the question seemed to be answered, with a degree of finality, as they closed the hatch behind me.

The engines were started and while Geoff was running them up and testing I got settled in my position. I pinned the chart to my table because I intended to keep an air plot going at least for the period when we would be out of sight of land. I checked that the W/T receiver was tuned to the correct frequency and I back tuned the transmitter to it. Then I checked that the rear gun was cocked and ready for instant action if needed. By this time we had moved away from the dispersal point and were trundling along the taxi track. I heard Geoff get clearance on R/T to take-off and he moved into position at the end of the runway.

"O.K. for take-off Denny?" he said, as he usually did.

"Yes," I replied and reminded him, "as soon as you can, turn port and climb on 235 degrees." This would take us to Lands End, where we had agreed to set course over Longships lighthouse.

As Geoff opened the throttles I heard the roar from the two Hercules engines and felt the surge of power as we gathered speed. We had done some forty take-offs together in Beaufighters and I was familiar with the sounds, vibrations and sensations, but this time it seemed different. For one thing, I was used to being able to see what Geoff was doing as he moved a hand to operate undercarriage, flap levers or throttles, etc. But because of the rocket rails, other equipment and kit stowed in the fuselage I could only just see the back of his head. It felt rather claustrophobic in the back. The weight of this freight blocking my view was probably well within the limit of the aircraft's capability, but psychologically it gave me the feeling that it was overloaded. It seemed that we were now going very fast but we had not yet lifted off. The runway here at Portreath was quite long, but surely we must be nearly at the end?

Recalling that beyond the end was the cliff-top with a sheer drop onto the rocks and sea below sent fearsome thoughts racing through my mind. Was there some problem preventing Geoff from getting airborne? Was there still some ice on vital wing surfaces? Was the plane too heavily laden? But I needn't have worried. At that moment I felt us lift off and then heard the undercarriage coming up. Maybe it was the proximity of the snow piled up at the edges of the runway that had given me the illusion that we had reached take-off speed sooner than we really had. I jotted down the time of take-off, 0700 hours and we were on our way with the first stage of that 7,000 mile journey.

By the time Geoff had completed a slow, climbing turn we were about two miles out to sea, but the heading I had given would cause us to converge with the coastline again. We crossed it over St. Ives, a compact little town with a small harbour. It looked beautiful in the bright sunshine. The surrounding countryside was covered with snow, there was snow on the roofs of the buildings in the town, and on a small beach adjacent to the harbour there was even snow extending down to the sea, where it was being melted by the lapping water from breaking waves. I had never been to Cornwall before and I remember thinking that St. Ives must be a very picturesque place in summer.

We flew on over the wintry landscape for about five minutes until we came to Lands End. Here, over Longships lighthouse, we set course for a calculated position of 48° 30'N, 9° 30'W in the open sea. We were now at about 4,000 feet and above scattered cumulus clouds. At intervals I could see Longships lighthouse slipping away into the distance. I had a bearing compass with me and was able to take a back bearing on it, which gave me a check on track made good. As it was finally lost from view I realised that it was my last look at the UK, and that I did not know how long it would be before I saw it again – or if I ever would.

There were some patches of cirrus cloud above but it was mostly blue sky and sunshine. Ahead the amount of cumulus cloud below us was increasing, just as the meteorological report had forecast. This was slightly annoying because by the time we should have been passing over the Scilly Isles I could see nothing. Then, by a stroke of luck, I spotted Bishops' Rock lighthouse below us through a small gap in the clouds. This pinpoint gave me a check on both track and ground speed and enabled me to calculate a wind velocity more accurate than the forecast one. Satisfied that we were on track, I swivelled my seat round to face backwards and concentrated on keeping a lookout.

We were flying just above the clouds so that we could quickly take cover in them if necessary. However this did make it more of a strain scanning the sky. The bright sun, still rather low in the sky behind us, was casting shadows on and between the billowing cloud tops. Several times I thought I saw another aircraft as a movement of a sharp shadow caught my eye. I had to keep alert but I was feeling safer by the minute as we drew further and further from the French coast.

After about an hour, we reached the ETA for my calculated position and turned onto a southerly heading. We were now about 250 miles from the French coast and would continue on this course for nearly two hours until we made landfall off Cape Finistere on the northwest corner of Spain. The Met report had forecast that the clouds would break up before we got that far and I had nothing to do now but to keep watch. Understandably, I was tending to spend more time looking out of the port side, in the direction of France, from where one might expect any enemy aircraft to come. It therefore came as a bit of a shock when I looked out of the starboard side and saw what appeared to be a single-engined aircraft. It emerged from behind one cloud top and was silhouetted against another. It was flying straight and level, heading towards France. This was no shadow!

"There's a single-engined aircraft on the starboard quarter, about 800 yards away," I called out to Geoff.

"Right," he said, "I'll drop down into cloud." He would not have been able to turn round far enough to see it himself anyway, without banking, so he wisely decided to seek cloud cover immediately. Then he began plying me with questions about it, but I had seen it so briefly that I could only say that it was a single-engined plane with a blunt nose shape characteristic of a radial engine. The significance of this was that the only German fighter it could have been was a Fw.190.

"But surely we are out of range?" he said. "How sure are you of our position?"

I replied that I was reasonably certain, but doubts began to creep into my mind. Had I made some ghastly error? Were we much nearer to the French coast than I thought? I checked the tracks on my chart, the courses we had flown and the times. No, I must be right, but time would tell...

We flew on in cloud. In the dull greyness it felt cool and humid but I had an eerie feeling that we were being watched. Had that German pilot seen us and was he shadowing us? I tried to convince myself that this was not possible. After about thirty minutes the cloud began to get thinner. I got occasional glimpses of blue sky above and patches of sea below until finally the clouds began to break up altogether. As we emerged into clear weather I took a good look around and was relieved to find that there was no other aircraft in sight anywhere. I was able to relax a bit. I drank some water from my water bottle and started to eat a piece of chocolate.

This mundane action seemed to trigger a sudden awareness of how far from mundane my experience at this moment really was. What was I doing, suspended in this confined cockpit some 4,000 feet above the sea, which stretched as far as the eye could see in all directions? I could see no land, no ships, no other planes and not even a bird. I felt isolated. I had a chart with a track marked on it which indicated that if we continued in this direction we would eventually reach land. But would we? I felt a bit like Columbus must have done!

We droned on, without much conversation, until suddenly Geoff called out, "I think I can see land on the port bow!" I swivelled my seat round and craned my neck to see forwards. Sure enough, there it was, a faint, thin smudge on the horizon. Patiently I waited, as we slowly got nearer and nearer until, about three minutes before our ETA, I was able to identify the promontory of Cape Finistere itself. There had been nothing wrong with my navigation. We altered course, in accordance with my flight plan, to take us down the coast of Spain and Portugal. I took two bearings on the Cape to get a running fix, mainly to establish that our distance from the shore was sufficient to avoid any infringement of territorial waters.

As I looked at my watch I could hardly believe that we had only been airborne for two hours and forty-five minutes and were still not quite half way to our destination. Ahead was 450 miles of flying down the coast to Cape St. Vincent at the southern end of Portugal but there was no longer any threat from enemy aircraft, we were only a few miles from a friendly coastline and the weather was fine. This part of the trip would be more pleasant, I thought, and so it was, from a scenic point of view, but by the time we drew level with the town of Oporto, which I could see clearly with its light coloured buildings bathed in sunshine, I was beginning to feel uncomfortably warm. Geoff too complained of the heat but there was nothing we could do about it.

We were in winter clothing but it was getting warmer by the minute. The main problem was the thick polo neck Guernsey sweaters we were wearing. To get them off would mean removing parachute harness, lifejacket and battledress top completely and then struggling to remove the sweater within a very confined space. This would be almost impossible and inadvisable to attempt in flight anyway.

Some forty minutes later, when we were near Lisbon, it got even hotter and we were both sweating. How nice it would have been if we could have landed there at the civilian airport, even just to change clothes and get iced drinks. But recalling the remarks of that briefing officer at Portreath, I don't think that this would have been accepted as a valid reason for getting interned! We had no alternative but to press on regardless of our discomfort.

Eventually we reached and rounded Cape St. Vincent on to a south easterly heading towards Rabat on the Moroccan coast. Less than an hour to go now... The southern coastline of Portugal was now diverging away from us on our left and soon we were out of sight of land again for a short while. We were still at 4,000 feet in sunshine and with clear blue sky above. The wind was now very light and the sea calm. Everything was fine, except that it was getting even hotter. When we first sighted land, at about 40 miles distant, Geoff began a slow descent, which increased our ground speed a little. If we could bring forward our landing time even by a few minutes it would be a relief.

We were down to 1,500 feet as we crossed the coastline at a point between Rabat and the smaller town of Sale. It was surprisingly hazy at low-level and it took us two or three minutes to locate the airfield, which was nearer to Sale. There was only one runway and thankfully there was no delay in getting clearance to land. As Geoff made his approach I could see unfamiliar palm trees, exotic looking shrubs and reddish soil – we were in a foreign land.

It wasn't one of his best landings. We bounced and then as we made contact again there was a strange rumbling noise. Then, as the tail came down I was alarmed by an abnormal clattering at the back. I thought that the tail wheel tyre must have burst.

"Sorry about that," said Geoff, referring to the landing. "This metal runway put me off." It was only then I realised that the runway was constructed of large interlocking steel plates. The plates were perforated with holes about six inches in diameter, which had caused the rumbling and vibration as the tyres ran over them. It was like driving a car over cobblestones. It was the first time we had landed on such a runway, although we were to become quite familiar with them in the months to come.

We had landed at 1300 hours, giving us a flight time of exactly six hours. This was the longest time Geoff and I had been airborne in a Beaufighter, or indeed any other aircraft to date. As we taxied to a dispersal point, the heat was almost unbearable. As soon as we stopped and the hatches were opened we almost poured out of the aircraft! We stood beside it, flinging off parachute harnesses, lifejackets, battledress tops, etc, in order to peel off those heavy sweaters. This was much to the amusement of the groundcrew who, needless to say, wore only khaki shorts and bush hats. They did not seem to have heard about the snow in Cornwall. We had to get all our kit out of the aircraft because we would need to unpack our tropical clothes, but for the moment we were driven off to the briefing room, rather incongruously dressed in thick blue serge trousers with braces, blue shirts without any tie and, most ridiculous of all, fur-lined flying boots!

Debriefing was a formality. I had almost forgotten sighting the 'Fw.190' but Geoff mentioned it and so I had to tell them about it. I gave them the time and position where I had seen it, but when I described it as having a single radial engine they looked dubious. It was too far out to sea for it to have been an Fw.190, they insisted. Nevertheless, they made a note of what I said, but I got the impression that they thought I had been mistaken in what I had seen. Even I was beginning to wonder if I had imagined it.

We were then taken to our respective accommodation. In my case it was a long, whitewashed chalet type of building with a veranda along the front, which overlooked a lawn surrounded by shrubs. It was, in fact, a row of single rooms, like cubicles, opening directly on to the veranda but with no doors, just curtains. It was probably intended as some sort of holiday accommodation because it was not far from the sea. There was a wash room at the end of the veranda and my first priority was to have a shower. It was glorious. Then I put on more appropriate clothing – khaki slacks and a shirt with sleeves rolled up. I knew I had things to do like re-organising my kit, packing away items like battledress, flying boots, etc, but I decided to lay on the bed and rest for a minute. That was a mistake. Not only did I miss lunch in the Mess but I nearly missed the evening meal as well because it was 5pm before I woke up.

I could hardly credit that this was the same day that I had awakened at five a.m. in a freezing cold Nissen hut in Portreath, feeling dreadful. Now I was in warm, sunny Morocco and feeling much better, even the ache in my arm was scarcely noticeable. After sundown I went for a walk in the balmy night air, which was heavy with the scents of unfamiliar shrubs, and reflected on the day. We had flown some 1,250 miles on the first and most dangerous part of our journey, but there were still about 5,750 miles to go. However, this would be done in easy stages over the next few days. Our itinerary – Biscra, Cairo, Bagdad, Bahrain, Karachi, Allahabad – sounded like a grand tour and promised to be an interesting experience which, in some ways, we were lucky to be having.

Except that, at the end of it all, we were going to war…

3. The 7,000 mile Journey Part II ~ Rabat to Allahabad

During the first part of our journey we had run the gauntlet across the Bay of Biscay, with the potential danger of enemy activity. We had a scare at sighting what I believed was a FW.190 German fighter. We had made our longest flight yet in a Beaufighter. During this six-hour flight we had experienced the extremes of temperature and humidity from cold wet snowy Cornwall to sweltering hot, sunny Morocco without even being able to change our clothes, and all this with a very sore arm suffering from a touch of Typhus! It was therefore likely that the rest of the journey, in easy stages across North Africa to the Middle East and on to India would seem somewhat of an anti-climax. Indeed, to use an RAF expression, it promised to be 'a bit of a doddle'. In some ways it was, but there were some events, and things I saw, that formed lasting impressions.

The day after we had landed at Rabat we did not fly. Our Beaufighter – NE.534 – had to be inspected and we had various things to attend to. I felt a bit selfconscious walking about in tropical kit – khaki drill bush jacket, shorts, socks, shoes and a bush hat. Of course everyone else was dressed the same but by comparison with them my knees and bare arms seemed to glow lily white. I did visit the stores and was able to get rid of some now unnecessary items such as fur lined flying boots and (somewhat reluctantly) my white Guernsey aircrew sweater.

We visited the briefing room to get some general information about our onward flight to Cairo. I was given a set of topographical maps but when I asked about a Mercator chart for the area they said, with an air of don't-you-know-there's-a-war-on, that they couldn't spare any for ferry crews. Topographical maps would have to do, they said. I was given information on frequencies and call signs of several wireless stations at airfields en route, including places like Tripoli, Benghazi and Tobruk. These names were familiar enough to me from news reports during the earlier battles in the Western Desert but I never thought I would be flying near them. However, the whole of this part of North Africa had now been cleared of enemy forces and there was no risk of hostile action.

Rabat to Biscra

On the morning of the 10th of March it seemed so strange turning up to board our aircraft dressed in this still unfamiliar tropical kit. We took off and flew towards our first destination, which was an airfield near the town of Biscra in Algeria. It was a bright sunny day with just a few scattered cumulus clouds.

I suppose in my mind I had expected Morocco to be mostly flat, unfertile sand but the terrain below, as we followed the railway to Fez and then on to Taza, was quite different to what I had imagined. There were green, cultivated fields, palm trees and other lush vegetation and where we could see the soil it looked reddish and fertile. And, far from being flat, we could see on our starboard side that we were converging with a range of hills known as the Middle Atlas, which stretched as far as Taza. After the pass at Taza we took a slightly circuitous route, as we had been briefed to do, to avoid flying over the highest peaks. We were now flying over more rugged terrain and close to the main Atlas range. The panoramic view of the mountains was breathtaking. There were many high peaks (according to my map the highest in the range was 7,330 feet) and a few had snow on them. I remember how weird it seemed that, sweltering in the heat of the near mid-day sun in the cockpit of that Beaufighter, I could see snow less than twenty miles away.

We flew on and landed without incident at Biscra, which was at the end of the mountain range. It was down nearer to sea level and on the edge of the Sahara desert, which lay to the south of it. We were to stay overnight here and when we were driven into the town I was surprised to find that we were to stay in a hotel which not only was being run by civilian staff but also was being used for both officers and senior NCOs. So here, at least, Geoff and I were staying in the same accommodation.

I had 'crewed up' with Geoff in the summer of 1943 at No.32 OTU on Vancouver Island in Canada. On our course there were pilots and navigators both commissioned officers and NCOs. Prior to the official crewing up meeting, there had been much discussion amongst us navigators in the NCOs Mess as to whether it was better to fly with an officer pilot or an NCO pilot of more equal rank. There were two schools of thought. Some said that although the pilot is always in command of an aircraft, whatever his rank, it was better to have an officer so that his authority as regards making decisions and giving orders was clear cut. Others thought that it was better to choose an NCO pilot so you would be living in the same Mess, drinking and socialising together and so getting to know each other really well – but here lay a danger that over familiarisation might lead to conflict in the air when, perhaps, emergency decisions had to be made.

I had decided to opt for having a commissioned officer as my pilot and so I bided my time until the official 'crewing' meeting. I was introduced to Geoff, then of Pilot Officer rank, who was one of a small group who did not yet have navigators. After quite a short conversation I decided that I liked him. He must have thought that I would be suitable and we crewed up together. Not socialising much when off duty was never a problem in Canada. I had three NCO navigator buddies (who also had officer pilots) with whom I went about much of the time. But back in the UK at Crosby-on-Eden (where I was separated from my former friends) and when in transit (as Geoff and I were now) it was sometimes a bit irksome not being in the same Mess or staying in the same accommodation. But it had been my choice...

Although we did not have time to see much of picturesque Biscra, which, before the war, I understood had been a popular holiday resort for the rich, we were able to take a stroll along the bustling street outside the hotel in the late afternoon and it was fascinating. There was a cosmopolitan air about the place. The local Algerians spoke Arabic or French but there seemed to be quite a few people of other nationalities and also many British army personnel, probably mostly on leave.

Back at the hotel we had dinner and then sat at a long bar which ran almost the length of the dining area. Geoff had struck up a conversation with two army officers. I had a couple of drinks with them and then went upstairs to study my maps before going to bed. We had decided to fly to Cairo in one hop. The distance was 1,300 miles which was almost the maximum range of the Beaufighter and would take about seven hours. It was going to be a long day.

Biscra to Marble Arch

The next morning I was down to breakfast early and had almost finished before Geoff appeared. He didn't eat much and said he felt a bit under the weather. Then we had to wait for our transport, which was late, and when we finally arrived at the airfield and boarded our aircraft we took off an hour later than we had planned. This was not a good start to the day. We had been briefed not to fly to Cairo directly, as this would take us a few miles offshore in the region of Benghazi and Tobruk, which we had been instructed to keep away from. Instead we set course initially for a staging post in the desert called Marble Arch, which was well inland from Tobruk. We would overfly Marble Arch then alter course a few degrees to port to take us to Cairo.

To begin with we were flying roughly parallel to the coastline, but about 20 miles inland. Visibility was good and I could still see the sea and the town of Tripoli in the distance. About an hour into the flight I suddenly caught the whiff of a cigarette.

"Are you smoking?" I asked Geoff, in what must have sounded like an accusing voice.

"Oh, sorry," he replied. "I should have told you!"

Pilots who were smokers like Geoff did sometimes have a cigarette whilst flying but he always told me if he was going to smoke, perhaps because he knew I didn't really approve. The fact that he felt the need for a cigarette confirmed my belief that he was feeling a bit off colour.

As we flew on, the coastline curved away from our track. We could no longer see the sea and the terrain below became more featureless desert. Then we began to see signs of the aftermath of recent battles. Burnt out tanks, wrecked trucks, armoured cars and abandoned artillery lay scattered in the sand. They were poignant reminders that Allied soldiers had died here to achieve the first major land victory of the war.

Before we reached Marble Arch we had some discussion as to whether we should land there and refuel as a precaution but because we had been late leaving Biscra, Geoff was afraid that we might be further delayed while they refuelled us and we would not get to Cairo West before sunset. He asked me again what our ETA was for Cairo West and what time I had been given for sunset. In this part of the world there was only a very short twilight period between sunset and nightfall, and he was not too keen on having to make a night landing at an unfamiliar airfield. I confirmed to him that we should arrive about 15 minutes before sunset and our overall flight time would leave us with a fuel margin for a further 25 minutes flying time. There was virtually no wind and so far we had maintained our intended track and groundspeed without any problem. He decided to fly on.

In due course we flew over Marble Arch and altered course a few degrees to port, heading for Cairo West. Marble Arch was just a runway and a collection of camouflaged buildings and tents in the middle of nowhere. It was surrounded by slightly undulating areas of greyish sand, interspersed with large patches of scrub vegetation, while to the south it merged into more typical barren yellow dunes. I don't think there had ever been a village here. I understood the place got it's name from an actual marble arch which had been built a few miles away, marking the beginning (or end!) of a road across the Libyan section of desert.

When we had passed over the airfield, Geoff had tried to make contact by R/T, as a matter of courtesy, to report that we had overflown them en route to Cairo. But he could not make contact and after about ten minutes he said that there seemed to be an electrical fault on his transmitter. He asked me if my W/T set was OK. I tried it and it was not working, although it had been when we set off from Biscra. There was no power to either set and we concluded that there must be a fault on the generator. In retrospect, I think we should have turned back immediately and landed at Marble Arch, however, Geoff decided that we should carry on. The only problem would be that he would not be able to talk to flying control when making our landing at Cairo.

As we flew on, there was more evidence of the aftermath of the battles that had taken place in the Libyan Desert. Then, as we entered the Egyptian sector, I saw below an even more desolate area of salty swamps, known as the Qattara Depression. I had heard about this extensive area, which was mostly below sea level and was almost impassable by wheeled and even tracked vehicles. I was gazing in awe at this terrain below when Geoff suddenly said, "Have we passed the critical point yet Denny?"

He meant the point beyond which it would be quicker to fly on to Cairo than to return to Marble Arch.

"Not yet," I replied, "it will be in about five minutes."

I was somewhat taken aback when he then said, "I want to turn back." He went on to say that he was having second thoughts about arriving at Cairo short of fuel with only about ten minutes daylight left and now no radio contact.

I gave him a course to steer for a reciprocal track. The weather was still calm with virtually no wind, and drift was negligible. Less blue sky was visible above, due to high levels of cirrus cloud making it seem duller, although the sun was still quite bright, low on the western horizon. Visibility, however, was still about 20 miles and I did not anticipate any problem in finding the airstrip and camp. We had been flying at around 5,000 feet, but about five minutes before ETA, Geoff started to reduce height in preparation for making a quick landing. On ETA we were down to about 2,000 feet – but there was no sign of the landing strip or buildings. We flew on for two or three more minutes, both of us looking all round. Then he started circling to the south, thinking he had seen it, but it was just another patch of scrub.

"I can't see it anywhere," he said. "What's gone wrong Denny?"

Even as he spoke, I felt a wave of panic, because I was wondering the same thing. This was a navigator's nightmare. Two minutes past ETA and our destination was nowhere in sight, yet visibility was a good fifteen miles. We were over featureless desert with only a limited amount of fuel left, no wireless contact and nightfall only fifteen minutes away. Had I given Geoff the wrong course? No, I was sure I hadn't. I remembered that less than half an hour ago I had recognised the two burnt-out German tanks that we had flown over when going in the other direction, therefore we must have been returning near enough along the right track. But, more urgently, what should I do now?

My mind momentarily slipped back to Navigation School. I recalled two things they told us *not* to do in such a situation as we were in – *'don't panic'* and *'don't circle aimlessly'*. But I was already beginning to panic and Geoff was starting to circle! The Air Navigation Manual recommends immediately starting a Square Search. This is a methodical search by flying tracks at right angles to each other, and a distance apart equal to twice the visibility. The first track can be in any direction and of length equal to twice the visibility. After the first ninety degree turn, the length of subsequent tracks flown should be increased by twice the visibility on every alternate track. However, I foresaw two potential problems. First, it was important to plot the courses so that at least I would be able to work out an approximate DR position if we abandoned the search. I would have to plot on the topographical map (more awkward and time consuming than on a chart) which would waste valuable minutes with my attention inside my cockpit instead of looking out. Secondly, the thoroughness of this search depends on a fairly accurate assessment of visibility. This would be alright to begin with but very soon visibility would start to diminish rapidly. How could I allow for this I wondered, but I had to do something quickly.

"I'm sure we are not far away from it," I said to Geoff, "but rather than circle we had better do a proper square search." He agreed and we started by turning due north. After my calculated time we turned due east and then, after a few minutes, and to my intense relief, Geoff cried out, "I can see it now, about five miles on our starboard bow!" He turned towards it, putting the undercarriage down and did a complete circuit round the airstrip at 1,500 feet to indicate that we wanted to land.

Whilst he was doing this, I was able to sit back and take a good look around and I realised why we had not spotted the landing strip earlier. We had probably passed about three miles south of it a few minutes before ETA but had not seen it because the area now looked very different to what it had done when we had passed over it before in bright sunshine. The undulating ridges and patches of vegetation were throwing long shadows from the red sun now sinking very low in the west. In fact, the whole area looked rather like a camouflaged groundsheet.

On the second time round, Geoff made a normal approach and got a green light to land. It was great to be safely down, and it was not a moment too soon, because this airstrip was not equipped for night flying.

Obviously, we would have to stay overnight, and here we would be in separate accommodation again. Geoff went to the Officers' Mess and I was taken to the NCOs' Mess. The sergeant who took charge of me said, somewhat apologetically, "I'm afraid we are in tents here. Come on, I'll show you." He led me to a tent at the end of a row, which had two beds in it but was unoccupied. He then went and got me a hurricane lamp and some matches, saying that I would need them later. I noticed that the bed had a mosquito net and I asked whether I would need to use it. "Well, it's too dry for mosquitoes," he said, "but I advise you to roll it down anyway ... unless, of course, you like rats!"

I thought he was joking but I found out later that he wasn't.

After the evening meal I stayed in the Mess for a while and then, by the aid of my hurricane lamp, I found my way to the tent and got into bed. It was very quiet and I was looking forward to a good night's sleep. But it was not to be. After about half an hour, scratching and scrabbling sounds began. I had a small hand torch and when I shone it out through the net I saw them... Several rats were running about in the tent, on the floor, on the other bed, on my haversack, up the canvas walls and indeed they seemed to be everywhere. They were big brown ones and when I say 'big' I mean BIG! So these were the notorious Desert Rats the Eighth Army had talked about. I suppose the personnel stationed here soon got used to them but it took me ages to get to sleep. When I woke, in the early hours of the morning, the noise had died down. Probably the rats had moved on, as they had not found anything edible. Then I became aware of another sound, a sort of pitter-patter on the canvas, like rain falling. It couldn't be rain, I thought, because I'm in the desert.

But I was wrong. When it got light and I ventured out, I found it was indeed rain. It was not raining much, but big drops were falling on the greyish sand, dampening it and giving rise to a rather unpleasant, dank smell. Talking to some of the others, I gathered that in this region the average rainfall was only about two or three inches a year, so what I had experienced on my one and only night in the Western Desert was quite a rare event.

Marble Arch to Cairo West

After breakfast next morning, 12th March, I met up with Geoff and we went out to our aircraft. Groundcrew were already working on it but the news was not good. The electrician said a generator fault was causing the problem and it needed to be replaced, but they didn't have another one. They had made a temporary alteration that would enable Geoff to use his R/T set and suggested that we fly on to Cairo, where they had far superior maintenance facilities and would probably be able to fit a new generator.

By the time we took off, the rain had gone and any patches of stratus cloud had disappeared in the heat of the sun. As we climbed on course for Cairo again I had a feeling of *déjà vu* as we flew over those same two burnt-out German tanks – a useful landmark unwittingly provided by some unfortunate Germans.

The flight was uneventful as we passed over the Qattara Depression and began to descend towards Cairo West airfield. Now that Geoff had the runway in sight, I had a few minutes to look around. Beyond the airfield I could see the sprawling city of Cairo. Then I turned my head to the left and got a quite a shock, because I was not expecting to see them – the three Great Pyramids of Giza. I had not realised that they were so near to the city. Veiled in a slight haze, they stood there in the desert as ghostly reminders of a past civilisation. It was awe inspiring to think that of the thousands of men who had built them, none could have imagined that some 5,000 years later ordinary mortals like me would be able to gaze down on them from above, like gods.

As soon as we had landed, we consulted the maintenance people. They agreed that the generator was faulty and must be replaced, indeed they would not clear the aircraft for the onward flight until this was done. But the bad news was that they did not have any spare generators. They sent a signal requesting one from the large stores and maintenance unit at Allahabad in India. Ironically, Allahabad was our destination, but we were to be stranded here in Cairo for the time being.

Transport Command aircraft from Allahabad frequently landed here en route to the UK and the generator would be on one of these, but they could not tell us when and we spent a frustrating few days hanging about waiting for it. Finally, it arrived on 15th March, but too late for us to start on the next stage of our flight to Habbaniya until the following day.

Cairo West to Habbaniya

On 16th of March we finally took off for Habbaniya and, as we climbed away on a course of about 070°, we crossed the Nile with the city of Cairo below. Looking backwards, I again saw the Pyramids, seeming even more ghostly than before in the morning haze. A short while later we crossed the Suez Canal at a point between Ismailia and Great Bitter Lake. Then we left civilisation behind for a while as our track took us along the northern edge of the Sinai Desert until we reached the town of Beersheba in Palestine. We were now flying at about 4,000 feet, with blue sky above but with considerable haze below, which limited visibility of the ground either side of us. This was particularly annoying as we flew on over the southern end of the Dead Sea, because the biblical town of Bethlehem was less than ten miles away on our left, but I didn't see it. We were now over Jordanian territory, which extended eastward, flanked by Syria to the north and Saudi Arabia to the south, neither of which we were allowed to fly over. We crossed the border, invisible except on my map, into Iraq. We were still flying over the desert, with few landmarks, until our track converged with an oil pipeline and road leading to the small town of Rutba. Here we altered course slightly for Habbaniya. The oil pipeline diverged away to the left but we could still see the road at intervals until we reached our destination.

Below us, vestiges of vegetation were increasing and there were a few clusters of small dwellings, but it was still mainly desert. Visibility had improved somewhat and about ten minutes before ETA we saw Lake Habbaniya, a large inland waterway about eleven miles long, and beyond it the convolutions of the Euphrates, glistening in the sun. We had no difficulty in locating the RAF station, which was situated in a bend of the river and about three miles from the lake. It was a very large complex of buildings, like a small township, with the runway just alongside.

I didn't know that it was a peacetime base (built in the 1930s under an Anglo-Iraqi treaty) but as Geoff came in to land I got at a good look at it and was amazed. There were numerous buildings of substantial brick construction – hangers, workshops, administration buildings, barrack blocks, etc – set out amongst a network of surfaced roads, trees, lawns and flower beds. There was no shortage of water here.

Later, after we had been driven to our respective Messes and I found accommodation in an NCOs block, I was even more amazed. Firstly, the accommodation was great. The bed was comfortable, the room seemed agreeably cool, in spite of the heat outside, and, wonder of wonders, there was an ablutions section at the end of the room with running water and flushing toilets. I gathered that whole complex had a proper sewerage system, albeit one that discharged into the Euphrates a couple of miles away.

When this remarkable RAF station was built in the late 1930s it was under terms of an Anglo-Iraqi treaty and it had no real military defences as such because it was in a 'friendly' country. It did have a high wire fence all round its seven-mile perimeter, but that was primarily to keep wandering local Iraqis out. But earlier during the war, in April 1941, there was a regime change in Baghdad, when the then Rashid Ali deposed the Regent, Abdulla Illah.

The new regime was more favourably disposed to the Germans than the British and suddenly found itself isolated in a hostile environment. For a while, the base was under siege from Iraqi soldiers and the heroic manner in which the air force personnel, together with the help of two or three companies of native Levies (British-trained Iraqi and Syrian troops who remained loyal) withstood the siege and eventually caused the Iraqi soldiers to withdraw is recorded in the annals of RAF history.

But it was what I was told about the sewerage system during this period that intrigued me. The system depended for its operation on a small pump house on the bank of the Euphrates. When hostile Iraqis took up positions along a slight escarpment overlooking the compound, they actually occupied the pump house building because it made a good observation and sniper post. But, astonishingly, the pumps were left running and the camp continued to enjoy the facilities of its sewerage system throughout the period of the siege. At the time the RAF personnel numbered about 1,200 and, together with the Levies and their families, other workers and some civilian refugees from there were around 10,000 people within the compound. Had the Iraqis the wit to switch off the pumps it would have made things very inconvenient (!) for the besieged.

Secondly, I was struck by how very English it all seemed. The roads had English names; I remember 'Cranwell Avenue' for example. Cranwell was a peacetime RAF station in the UK where I had done my wireless training and this place reminded me of it. But at Cranwell the Lecture Rooms and Barrack Blocks were mostly of wooden construction, whereas here everything was much grander. I had a really good night's sleep here; no rats to keep me awake, like my night in the desert at Marble Arch.

Habbaniya to Bahrain Island

Next morning, the 17th March, I met up with Geoff and we went out to our aircraft. It had been given its daily inspection and all was in order, so we took off on the next stage of our flight, which was to the RAF base on Bahrain Island, at the lower end of the Persian Gulf. As we climbed away from the runway, I took a last look back at this remarkable 'little bit of England' created in the Iraqi desert.

We could not fly in a direct line to Bahrain, as this would mean crossing a bit of Saudi territory. Instead, we took a south-easterly course down the centre of Iraq to Basra, at the southern end of the country. From Basra we proceeded to the Persian Gulf along a ten-mile 'corridor' of Iraqi land, flanked on our left by Iranian and on our right by Kuwaiti territory. Once over the Gulf, we were free to fly down the Saudi coastline, just offshore, all the way down to Bahrain Island.

If any part of this long journey, delivering a war machine and ourselves to the war, could be described as 'enjoyable' then this bit of the trip was it. The azure sky was cloudless, the sea was calm and blue and we were flying just off the shore with miles of deserted sandy beaches, golden in the bright sunshine. When we got to Bahrain, a small island about fifteen miles long by a few miles wide and as flat as a pancake, it seemed idyllic.

The air base was a mile or two from the town and we were both accommodated in a small hotel close to it, which was very comfortable. In the late afternoon we walked across a stretch of golden sand towards the sea. It was very hot but there was a gentle breeze, producing little wavelets. The flatness of the beach gave the illusion that we both remarked on, that the sea was higher than the land. We stood there for quite a while, fascinated by the tiny waves, which didn't break but gently lapped onto the very hot, dry sand until they just evaporated before our eyes. The sand was dry again in seconds. Walking back to the hotel, it was so warm, calm and peaceful that I would have liked to have stayed there forever.

But it was like the calm before the storm. The next stage of the flight would take us, in one hop, to Karachi, where we would be under South East Asia Air Command – and that much nearer to the war.

Bahrain Island to Karachi

When we took off next morning, the weather was again bright and sunny. We climbed to our usual height of around 4,000 feet, crossing the south end of the Gulf towards the peninsula of Oman. There was an RAF at station at Sharjar, which we would overfly and then turn eastwards over the Arabian Sea, keeping a few miles off the coastline, firstly of Iran and then of Pakistan, all the way to Karachi. It should have been straightforward but something happened that I hardly like to relate, because it made me look a complete fool and probably embarrassed Geoff too.

About ten miles before we reached the Omani coastline, I looked out and saw a flame coming from the trailing edge of the port wingtip. I told Geoff but he could not see it. On a Beaufighter, the port engine obstructed the vision of the pilot so that he could just about see the leading edge, but not the trailing edge, of the wingtip. Geoff was a bit alarmed and kept asking me to describe the flame. I told him it was about eighteen inches long, bluish, changing to orange and yellow tipped, and looked like an electrical fire. But the only electrical item at the wingtip was the navigation light and that was not switched on. Also, there should not be any fuel or combustible material in this region.

The possibility that it was Saint Elmo's Fire crossed my mind, but I dismissed it. It was the wrong colour, it looked too substantial, there were no signs of it from any other extremities or edges of the aircraft and it was in broad daylight. *Saint Elmo's Fire* is the name given to the discharge sometimes seen from pointed parts of an aircraft (or ships at sea – indeed the name Saint Elmo is a derivative of Saint Erasmus, the patron saint of sailors) when flying in an atmospheric electrical field. I had experienced it often in Canada at night or very occasionally in daytime gloom flying in or around snowstorms. Also, I had seen a very violent display of it over the Irish Sea one dark and stormy night. The 'flames' are predominantly blue, ethereal, and flickering or sometimes glowing like a halo round the propellers. But I had never seen it in broad daylight and cloudless skies.

The flame had now lengthened to about four feet and when I told Geoff he contacted Sharjar by R/T and said he wanted to make a precautionary landing as 'he might have a small fire on board' as he put it. They responded immediately, saying that the airfield was clear and he could come straight in. I was keeping a nervous eye on the flame, which started to shorten back a bit as Geoff began to descend quite rapidly and our speed increased. By the time we were down to 1,500 feet and were approaching the runway the flame had disappeared.

As soon as we turned off the runway we stopped and got out. We were met by the groundcrew and a fire engine.

"Where's the fire?" everyone was asking. But there was no fire. I explained about the 'flame' I had seen coming from the wingtip, but there was no visible sign of any damage. They got a stepladder and examined the wingtip more closely, but there was no sign of any scorch marks or anything to indicate that there had been any heat present. I went up the ladder myself and had to agree.

I felt an absolute idiot! Geoff also must have felt embarrassed that he had made an emergency landing for no apparent reason but he was philosophical about it and said that it was better to have been safe than sorry. We concluded that it must have been some manifestation, akin to St. Elmo's fire, that can happen even in fine hot weather in these more tropical conditions.

An electrician did a few checks, but everything was in order. They topped up our fuel and we climbed aboard – in my case somewhat sheepishly because I felt that behind my back they were winking and nudging one another with mutterings of 'fresh out from Blighty' or 'not used to the heat' and 'seeing things', etc. I was glad when we took off and set course eastwards over Arabian Sea, leaving that incident behind us.

It was still a beautiful day. We flew two or three miles off the rocky coastline, with impressive mountain ranges rising far into the distance. First it was Iranian territory and later that of Pakistan, all the way to Karachi in India, where we landed. The airfield (Mauripur Road) was quite a busy one, with Transport Command aircraft frequently arriving and leaving. We were to stay here overnight.

I was taken to an NCOs' Mess, which was probably one of several, because it seemed to be primarily for itinerant aircrew. It was small, cosy and had white tablecloths. What luxury! Accommodation was in a row of bamboo Bashas nearby. I was in one by myself. It had just one charpoy-type bed and electric light, albeit from a bare bulb hanging from the ceiling. About dusk I went to the Mess. It was about 150 yards along an unlit track and, anticipating that it would be dark when I when I came out, I left the light on to make it easier to find my way back. That was a mistake – but an even bigger mistake was that I didn't fix the mosquito net because I didn't think it was necessary at this time of the year.

The meal in the Mess was good and I stayed there quite some time because there were people to talk to. Then, when I eventually went back, the light certainly made it easier for me to find my way along the track, but when I went inside I got a shock. I was aghast to find a mass of winged insects gyrating around the bare lightbulb. There were moths and flying beetles of all shapes and sizes and many other queer airborne creatures I had never seen before, but even worse, the top cover sheet of my bed was crawling with buzzing, half-dead casualties of collisions with the hot bulb. It was a nightmare.

First I had to switch the light off for a while, to try and disperse the throng. Then it took me ages to repeatedly shake out and brush the bed cover until I finally fixed the mosquito net and got into bed.

I lay there for a while, thinking that this had not been my day – but at least I had learned a couple of things about being 'out East'. Firstly, if you see a flame streaming from a wingtip, ignore it! Secondly, *always* make sure your mosquito net is down before dark; even if there are no mosquitoes about, there are other things that go buzz in the night.

Perhaps tomorrow would be a better day. The final day of our journey from here to Allahabad should be straightforward – or so I thought.

Karachi to Allahabad

Next morning we were down at the flight office bright and early, only to be greeted by bad news. They had discovered another fault on our aircraft. I don't remember the details but they needed another replacement component, which they did not have. Again, they would have to wait for delivery from Allahabad. It was Cairo all over again and we would have to hang about, bored and frustrated, for several days.

But there was a difference... we were now officially in South East Asia Air Command and I think someone realised that, although NE.534 was temporarily grounded, its aircrew were not. We were told that we were urgently needed for operational flying and should report to Allahabad as soon as possible. They might have sent us on by train, but then someone remembered that there was another Beaufighter, NE.253, which, for some reason, was waiting to be returned to Allahabad. We were asked to take it.

I felt a bit disappointed that we were going to have to 'change horses' and not get to fly NE.534 all the way, but we had no choice.

Accordingly, we took off in NE.253 on 23rd March. It was a routine flight, two thirds of the way across India, with one re-fuelling stop at Jodhpur. Thus we arrived at our destination of Allahabad, twenty days after leaving Portreath in the UK.

But we were still about 600 miles from the battlefront...

4.   Lonely Journey in a Foreign Land

We arrived at Allahabad on 23rd March. It was the end of our 7,000 mile air journey by Beaufighter and we now expected to be posted to an operational squadron. Here Geoff and I were in different living quarters and I found myself again feeling a bit isolated and lonely. For the first couple of days we met at the orderly room but they said that they were waiting for posting instructions to come through from 224 Group, which might not be for several days, and they would notify us when this happened.

I was in a hut with a dozen or more NCO aircrew but mostly they were in transit, just staying one or two nights, so it was not easy to get to know anyone. However, there was one crew who were resident because they were on the Ferry and Transport Unit. Their duties included flying replacement Beaufighters to the squadrons (and then returning as passengers in an Anson of a communications flight). I asked them what squadron they thought that Geoff and I would be posted to. They replied that it would most likely be 27 Squadron, currently at Cholavaram (near Madras), who were on coastal duties. The alternatives were 177 Squadron, who were at Feni, or 211 Squadron at Bhatpara (near Comilla). Both these latter squadrons were engaged on long-range offensive sorties at low-level over Burma. One of the ferry crew added jokingly, "You don't want to go to 211 Squadron. We always seem to be going there!" – the implication being that their return visits were because yet another Beaufighter and its crew had been lost.

Because our training, both in Canada and at Crosby-on-Eden, had been orientated towards operations over the sea, and we had not practised any low flying or air-to-ground strafing over land, it seemed most likely that we would go to 27 Squadron and I felt less apprehensive about this. What I did not know at the time was that 27 Squadron was at

Cholavaram temporarily 'on rest' after having been on operations over Burma continuously for fifteen months up to the end of 1943, and had suffered quite heavy losses.

After a few days I had a message from Geoff to say that he had reported sick with a skin infection and had been sent to the nearby military hospital for treatment and observation. This increased my feeling of loneliness and the next few days dragged on. I was having difficulty in getting used to the heat and spent most of the time just lying on my bed reading or writing letters. Then one day I decided that I must go into the town, even though I had nobody to go with. At the main gate there were usually rickshaws available, but I chickened out on using one because I didn't 'know the ropes' regarding payment etc, and I was still an obvious white knee'd newcomer. I took the RAF bus instead.

So I found myself in the bustling centre of a foreign city. It was a great culture shock. I had, of course, been abroad before, but that was in Canada, where virtually everybody spoke English. Even in the predominantly French provinces most people were bi-lingual and although many street signs, notices and shop-fronts were in French, I was able to understand them from what I had learned at school. I had not felt that I was in a 'foreign' country. But here in Allahabad I was surrounded by people who were speaking a language (indeed probably several languages) that I did not understand and street signs and notices, etc., that to me were meaningless squiggles. I was bewildered by the great diversity of traffic and people. On the roads were bicycles, rickshaws, handcarts, bullock carts, horse drawn carriages, ancient lorries and a few equally ancient motor cars and wooden buses. These contrasted sharply with the occasional modern jeep and other military vehicles. Motley crowds of people were milling about, mostly on the roads, dodging the hazards of the traffic. There were coolies and women carrying enormous loads on their heads, many men barefoot and wearing only loincloths, others more respectable, wearing dhotis and sandals, sometimes carrying sun umbrellas. There was a great variety of dress worn by the women also. Some looked poverty stricken, in little more than rags. Others wore more colourful saris and were usually not on foot but riding by in rickshaws or carriages.

But what shocked me most were the hoards of near-naked begging children. As a serviceman on my own, and an obvious newcomer as betrayed by my lack of sun tan, I seemed to be singled out wherever I went to be surrounded by them with their incessant cries of '*backsheesh Sahib*'. I wandered round for a while, looking at shops and street stalls. I bought a book on learning how to speak Hindustani, which proved to be useful later on. On my way back to where the pick-up point for the bus was, I stopped and joined a crowd who were watching a street magician. He was sitting cross-legged at one end of a reed mat. He had a flat, wooden, cut-out model of an Indian dancer, which was passed around to the crowd for them to look at. He then threw the doll onto the centre of the mat and proceeded to play a small flute, like a snake charmer. The doll stood up on end and jigged about, as though dancing. A small boy assistant walked round the doll to show that there were no wires or threads. When the flute playing was stopped the doll fell flat down and was picked up by the boy and passed round again for examination. I watched this done several times. I knew it must be a trick but I could not figure out how it was done, particularly with everyone watching so closely. On the other hand, I thought, I was in the land of the legendary Indian Rope Trick. Perhaps it *was* magic!

Back in the camp the next few days dragged on. I began to learn some words in Hindustani from the book I had bought. Also, in response to some questions I asked about Hindu 'religion' someone in the hut lent me a little book. But it dealt more with the roots of Hinduism in what seemed to be a rather intellectual and abstract manner. It described the concept of Brahman – the all embracing but unmanifest, attributeless 'one without a second'. I found it all rather difficult to grasp, particularly when I thought of the crowds of people, mostly Hindu, that I had seen in town and the numerous pictures and images of deities which they presumably worshipped. How did they relate to what I was reading and trying so hard to comprehend? Nevertheless, I can remember having a strong but ineffable feeling that I was on the verge of a great discovery (as indeed I probably was if I had just persevered with the book). In retrospect, I think it was a flash of expanded 'Inner Self' awareness, like that which I had experienced during the crash at Crosby-on-Eden and was also to experience subsequently during some of the more traumatic moments of operational flying.

But I never finished the book. After breakfast on the morning of April 14th I had just started reading again when an airman came with a message that I was to report to the Orderly Room. When I got there, the corporal at the desk took several minutes searching through a mass of papers until he finally came up with the words I least wanted to hear.

"Ah, Sergeant Spencer," he said. "You have been posted to No.211 Squadron." He asked me to come back in the afternoon to collect a railway warrant. I would be travelling by rail next morning from Allahabad to Calcutta, where I would report to the RAF Transit Camp for further travel instructions. I reminded him that my pilot, P/O Vardigans, was in the hospital and shouldn't I wait for him? But he said that the Adjutant dealt with officer postings and that I would have to go on ahead alone.

I decided that I must go and see Geoff. The military hospital was a bit out of the town centre and this time I was advised to go by rickshaw, which I did. This mode of transport was commonplace, but for me it was a new experience. We passed some comparatively grand buildings, one being the University, before coming to the hospital, which was itself quite a large, older-style, brick building. I paid the rickshaw wallah, probably too much, because he seemed pleased and did not haggle. I found Geoff, who was well enough, but bored. He hadn't been told about the posting yet and was not particularly worried that we would be involved in a low-level ground attack role. We had a chat, during which I mentioned that I was not looking forward to making the long train journey, of about 480 miles, to Calcutta by myself. He said that he was not in a position to ask for my departure to be delayed, particularly as he had been told that it would be about ten days before he would be discharged, and he said that I had best go on ahead as instructed. As I left he said, "Why don't you ask if there is any chance of getting a lift by air? It's worth a try."

Outside the hospital there were several rickshaws. I hailed one and set off back to the camp, this time feeling more confident, just like a seasoned burrah Sahib. Back in my hut I spoke to one of the resident aircrew about the possibility of getting a lift to Calcutta. He suggested that I should go and see one of the pilots on their Dakota flight, a W/O Keyes, whom he thought was taking a Dakota to Calcutta the very next morning. I sought out W/O Keyes, who proved to be a pleasant chap.

"No problem," he said. "You can come with us, provided that you don't mind sitting in the fuselage with the freight." He said that a truck would be picking him and his two crew members up at about 0800 hours, but his hut was some distance from mine and, when he realised that I would have two kit bags and a haversack, he said not to worry, they would come and pick me up from my door. I couldn't believe my luck. I had got it organised so easily but would probably not even have tried if it hadn't been for Geoff's suggestion.

Later that afternoon I went to the orderly room. The corporal at the desk gave me my travel documents and a railway warrant. When I told him that I didn't want the warrant because I had arranged to go by air he looked annoyed and disapproving.

"You're supposed to go by train," he muttered. "Getting a lift is unofficial. How do you know you can rely on the Dakota? You better take the warrant and be at the main gate at 0800 hours. Transport goes to the station every morning at that time."

To avoid further argument, I took the warrant and left, but I was determined to go by air. Then, when I got back to my hut, I began to have doubts. W/O Keyes had said they would pick me up at 'about' 0800 hours, but could I trust him not to forget? After all, this was an unofficial arrangement and if they did not turn up it would be too late for me to carry my kitbags down to the main gate, which was quite some distance away, to get the official transport to the railway station. If I missed the train I might be in serious trouble.

Next morning I was up early, got ready and was waiting at the door of my hut by 0745 hours. I had decided to rely on the Dakota crew. After all, the flight to Calcutta would only take about three hours, a much more attractive proposition than an eleven-hour train journey, arriving sometime in the middle of the night. But by 0810 nobody had arrived and I was beginning to get worried. Another nail-biting five minutes passed before, to my great relief, the truck arrived. I climbed on board and we all went to the briefing room. W/O Keyes filed his flight plan, I was noted down as a passenger, and we were then driven out to the aircraft. It was a Transport Command Dakota FL.627 and was only about half full of freight, mostly crates containing aircraft spares, so there was plenty of room. I found myself a seat on a small case by a window so that I could see out.

We took off at 0925 hours and climbed to about 3,000 feet. This was the first time I had flown in a Dakota and by comparison with Beaufighters, which normally cruised at 180 knots, it seemed slow and lumbering at around 135 knots. Apart from conditions, being rather bumpy, the flight was uneventful and we landed at Dum Dum, an airfield on the outskirts of Calcutta, at 1230 hours. Even here my luck was in, as it transpired that the Dakota crew were staying overnight in Calcutta and transport was provided to take them into town. W/O Keyes said it would only mean a slight detour for them to drop me off at the transit camp, which they did.

I could not see very much from the back of the truck but my first impression was of driving down a tree-lined avenue with some grand-looking houses on either side. They were set back, behind high walls and with imposing iron gates, through which I got glimpses of courtyards or shaded gardens with exotic shrubs and trees. The houses were mostly white-walled, with windows shuttered by green jalousies. Some of them looked as though they had seen better days but still appeared to be little havens of peace and tranquillity in that troubled city. But soon we began cutting through far less salubrious backstreets which were bustling with humanity.

Eventually, they dropped me off at a drab-looking brick building in an obviously commercial rather than residential street. Thus, in the early afternoon I found myself at my destination, without having had the hassle of that long train journey – but what a destination! It was a shambles. The building was probably originally a *godown* or warehouse of some sort. Accommodation, for airmen and NCOs alike, was in one large, long room, crammed with Indian-type charpoy beds. There was no separate NCOs mess, at least not for transient personnel like myself, and we ate in a large cafeteria type canteen. The reception area, where I had reported in, had a long counter with several staff but there always seemed to be queues of airmen seeking information and not getting it. The place seemed to be in a permanent state of confusion, indeed, it did not surprise me to hear a story that, only a few weeks previously, a group of airmen had been posted to RAF airstrips in the Manipur area, only to be told, when they got to Comilla, that these units were now in Japanese hands! They had been sent all the way back to Calcutta because no one had any instructions as to what they should do.

Up to this point I had been 'in transit' for 38 days since leaving the UK on 8th March and I began to realise, with some alarm, how little I knew about the war in South East Asia. Apparently, whilst I had been travelling, desperate battles had been in progress at Kohima and Imphal to prevent the northern thrust of the Japanese forces from crossing the Naga Hills and onto Indian soil. Imphal was only about 350 miles northeast of Calcutta. In fact, on this very day, the 16th April, that I was in this transit camp, both Kohima and Imphal were still encircled, although the sieges of both were relieved a few days later. But I did not know this at the time. I never saw an officer and nobody briefed me as to what was happening.

That afternoon I got my travel documents for the following morning. At breakfast I collected a small bag of 'rations' (two corned beef sandwiches and some awful biscuits) and was instructed to fill my water bottle with 'fresh' water from the canteen (heavily dosed with chlorine, which tasted more like chlorine lightly diluted with water). In due course, transport arrived to take me, the only NCO, and several airmen, to Howrah station. It was only as we crossed a multi-span girder bridge that I realised the station was not in the main part of the city but on the opposite bank of the Hoogli River. The station itself was a seething mass of humanity. I got instructions from the RTO as to which platform to go to and found that the train was, in fact, a troop train. It was all open plan third class carriages, dirty and already quite full up with squaddies. I was wondering whether there was any section set aside for NCOs when I saw three army sergeants, about the same age as myself, wandering up the platform. They said that I had best tag along with them and they 'commandeered' a space with four seats at one end of a carriage.

The train set off shortly before mid-day and trundled, painfully slowly, northwards. It was hot, uncomfortable and dreary. But at least I had the three sergeants to talk to. They couldn't tell me much about how the war was going because they just didn't know. However, they were able to explain to me about the journey. Since leaving Allahabad I had not had access to a map and I could not picture where we were going. I knew that Comilla was on the eastern side of the delta, that is the multiple mouths of the Ganges which flow into the Bay of Bengal, but I hadn't realised that there was no direct rail link because there were no bridges. We were going about 150 miles northwards to a place called Faridpur. Here we would get on a river steamer and come back southwards some 60 miles down interconnected navigable waterways, disembarking at Chandpur on the eastern side of the delta, where there was another rail link to Comilla and elsewhere.

It was early evening by the time we got to Faridpur and dusk as we boarded the river steamer. It was very crowded but the four of us stayed together and sat on kitbags at a vantage point by the handrail near the bows, although there was not much to see as darkness fell very soon after we got under way. There were hardly any lights to be seen, except those on the boat. There was a searchlight on the bow and another on the bridge. Frequently, instructions were shouted from the helmsman to the lookout on the bow, apparently for him to swing the searchlight from one side to the other. Most of the time we were travelling quite fast, maybe 12 knots or more, and I was intrigued as to how they were finding their way along this tortuous waterway amongst numerous sandbanks and small islands. Then I noticed that there were occasional marker buoys (without lights) which were located and held in the beam of the bow light until the helmsman instructed the lookout to search for the next one ahead.

Sometimes the throbbing of the engines reduced and we slackened speed. Perhaps it was a tricky stretch, or perhaps they had not located the next, maybe vital, buoy. With less noise from the engine the sounds of the night, croaking of bullfrogs, cries of wildfowl disturbed by the boat or by predators and other unidentifiable noises became more audible. In India the night is seldom silent. Travelling by river steamer at night was certainly a weird experience for me.

We disembarked at Chandpur around 0230 hours next morning. Not all of the service personnel on the steamer, including the three sergeants, were going to Comilla. I said goodbye to them and then, carrying my kitbags, I walked with a smaller group of soldiers a short distance to a railway siding where the train for Comilla was standing. It was shorter than the previous one, although with the same type of carriages, but older and even dirtier. Although it was dimly lit, I could see litter on the floor and occasionally cockroaches, big brown ones, scuttling across. Cockroaches on a train? Well, this was India, or to be more precise, East Bengal. I remember wondering how they got on and off the train, or did they spend their lives commuting between Chandpur and Comilla?

As there were fewer personnel on the train it was possible to find a seat to lie on. I dozed off once or twice but it was difficult to sleep, partly because the night air was surprisingly cold but mainly because of the way the train clanked and jolted along. It must have been a terrible track. Out of the windows I saw the first grey streaks of dawn and not long after, at about 0530 hours, we arrived at Comilla. I did not know how far away Bhatpara was, but I was relieved to find an RTO office in the foyer with an NCO on duty, even at this early hour. When I asked how I could get to No.211 squadron at Bhatpara he said, "That's easy. Their ration wagon comes into the market in Comilla every morning and always comes round here on the way back. But I'm afraid you will have a long wait, it doesn't usually get here until about 1000 hours." Then he added that he had seen another RAF sergeant who was going there and I would probably find him outside the front of the station.

I went outside. Just across the road, in front of the station, there was a small, green open space, where I saw an RAF sergeant sitting on a grass mound. He had his back to me and was hunched forward slightly, looking out across the green in a dejected manner, or so it appeared to me. I went and sat beside him and we introduced ourselves. He was Geoff Lowcock, a pilot already on 211 Squadron, but I will refer to him as just Lowcock to avoid confusion with my own pilot whose first name was also Geoff. He had not been on my train but had arrived by a different one from Ranchi. At first I thought he was returning from leave but later on he told me that he had been on a refresher course on handling Beaufighters. Apparently, while on the squadron he had landed short of the airfield and badly damaged the undercarriage on a Beaufighter. His airmanship had been judged to be at fault.

I think it was when he said, "but I'm all right now, I've got my confidence back," that I first sensed that this was not so. I was physically weary after my long lone journey from Allahabad but emotionally keyed-up because I was nearly at my destination – an operational squadron. Maybe this sharpened my perception, because I had a strange feeling of foreboding about him that I could not explain. I would not have wanted to fly with him as my pilot.

We had nowhere to go and nothing to do but wait for that wagon and we sat there and talked on and off about general things for hours. He seemed to be quite a nice chap and I cannot explain why I had this strange foreboding about him.

After what seemed like eternity – actually it was a bit over four hours – a three-ton RAF truck drove up. With the airman driver there was also a corporal from the catering section in the cab. He got out and helped us climb up into the back, which was quite high off the ground. Inside there were quite a few small crates and boxes of perishable foodstuffs, which we had to clamber over to get up front behind the cab. The latter had an open back, making some conversation possible. Judging by the banter between them, both the occupants in the cab seemed to know Lowcock quite well. The talk was mostly about people on the squadron that I did not know and I felt rather out of the conversation.

Bhatpara was about eighteen miles from Comilla but after the first few miles the road got progressively worse. The truck bounced and jolted over potholes and big stones, causing some of the smaller crates to dance about on the floor. I don't think we travelled at more than 15 mph throughout the whole journey and the noise required any conversation to be at near shouting level.

At one stage Lowcock asked, "Any more losses?"

"Yes," was the reply, "yesterday. Chambers and Lovell."

I clearly remember the tone of Lowcock's voice as he replied with a cry of, "Oh no! Not Skid Chambers". I guess that 'Skid' had been a buddy of his. Although the heat of the sun was now making itself felt through the canvas top of the truck, and it was beginning to get quite hot inside, I felt a shiver down my spine as I listened to those words. Of course I knew that I was joining an operational squadron, and I knew that there must be losses, but the reality of it was beginning to strike home.

It was about 1130 hours by the time we reached the camp. They dropped me and my kitbags off at the Sergeant's Mess. Lowcock said that I had best wait there for about half an hour, when all the NCOs would be coming in for lunch, and speak to the SWO (Station Warrant Officer) about accommodation. The Mess was a bamboo basha, which I thought was surprisingly small. I left my kitbags outside by the door and went in. After the noise and jolting of that ride in the truck, and the increasing heat of the sun, it was pleasantly quiet and relatively cool inside. There was a single room, almost square, with a row of built-in bamboo tables with form-type seats along two of the walls. The tables had white tablecloths and were set with cutlery, giving the empty room an unexpectedly welcoming atmosphere. There was a door with a curtain at the far end, which I guessed led to the cookhouse, and in the right hand corner by the door was a hatchway with a small counter, which obviously served as a bar.

Just as I was looking in that direction, the bar flap opened and I saw an airman, who was presumably acting as barman. He was surprised to see me and as soon as he realised that I was newly arrived he said, "Welcome to 211 Squadron." (he was the first person to do so) and offered me a bottle of beer 'on the house'. I sat on a stool and chatted to him for about half an hour until other NCOs began to drift in. They seemed a friendly lot and two of them suggested that I should sit with them and start lunch and they would tell me when the SWO came in. I well remember that first meal because I was starving hungry. It was what seemed to be corned beef soup, followed by corned beef fritters with some rather pathetic green vegetables, followed by stewed mangoes. I thought it was wonderful – but I did not know then that this would be virtually the same menu every lunchtime and, with some occasional variations such as a bit of mutton, for dinner also. Nor did I know that I would soon learn to hate corned beef and develop a lifelong aversion to mangoes, surely God's most tasteless fruit!

Soon the SWO came in. He took my papers and said that he would book in my arrival but I would not need to do anything until the next day when I should report to S/L Muller-Rowlands, the OC of 'B' Flight. He said the first thing was to find me some accommodation so that I could get some sleep. He then called out to someone on the other side of the room, "Sergeant Thomson, there's a spare bed in your basha isn't there?" Sergeant Thomson looked across at us and replied, in what seemed to be a very hesitant manner, "Er... well... er... yes I suppose there is." His hesitancy made me think that perhaps he didn't like the look of me as a new roommate, but he told the SWO that he would take me there after lunch.

Sergeant Thomson, whom I soon found out everyone normally called 'Tubby', was a pilot and he introduced me to his navigator 'China' Whale, who was also a sergeant.

Together they took me a short distance along a dust track that had a row of bamboo bashas along one side. They were smaller than those I had seen so far and were almost square, each housing three or four beds. Tubby warned me that the 'beds' were of rigid built-in construction, like the tables in the mess, but that once you got used to them they could be quite comfortable. Their basha was almost at the end of the row. As we went in the door I saw two beds on the right hand side and one on the left, which Tubby indicated would be mine. There were several items of kit strewn on the bed, which he began to collect up.

"It's alright," he said. "This isn't anybody's bed. This stuff is supposed to be in the stores. I'll put it in the corner for now and see to it later." But as he moved a kitbag that had been lying beside the bed my eyes focused, like a zoom lens, on the writing on it, which read *Sergeant R.A. Chambers.*

It was a dramatic moment as I realised that I was taking over the bed of someone who just the day before had been posted as 'missing believed killed'. Suddenly, I understood why Tubby had hesitated in the mess when he had been asked about a spare bed. He had been in the process of sorting out Chamber's service kit from any personal effects and knew that he had left items lying about on the bed which might lead me to ask questions; as it was, he had quietly moved the things away and I would have been none the wiser but for the fact that he did not know that I had already heard about Chambers during my ride in the ration wagon from Comilla. Nevertheless, I thought it was a kindly act on his part. Neither Tubby nor China ever mentioned Skid and, as I found out later, aircrews seldom talked about those who did not come back.

Tubby and China said they were going to walk to the airfield and would leave me to sleep for the afternoon undisturbed. Exhausted though I was, it took me a little while to go to sleep. This was not just because it was very hot or that the bed was unfamiliarly hard, but because my mind was in a turmoil. This last stage of the journey, without Geoff, had been a long and lonely one, in a land with a culture completely foreign to me. Nobody in authority had seemed to care about me. Now, at the end of my journey, I was trying to get to sleep in a bed that had belonged to someone who had been posted 'missing believed killed' only the previous day. But at least I was now on the squadron and I felt amongst friends.

My first impressions of the squadron, gained during the next few days and my first experience of operational flying are narrated elsewhere, but a strange thing was that I never saw Sergeant Lowcock around. I believe he was immediately posted to Poona, where there was a pool of unallocated aircrew. Indeed, I never saw him again, until fifteen months later, well after I had completed my tour of operations and left the squadron, when I happened to witness the last second of his life, as the Mosquito aircraft he was flying plummeted vertically into the ground.

Sequel

Geoff and I survived our tour of operations and in February 1945 we were posted separately to other units for our six months period of 'rest' from operational flying. I was sent to No.1672 MCU (Mosquito Conversion Unit) at Yelahanka near Bangalore, where I was on the staff as Navigation Officer. In practice, this post proved to be a bit of a sinecure. However, I did do some flying in twin-engined Oxford aircraft. The unit had several of these, which were used for training pilots who maybe needed some extra tuition on twin-engined machines before flying Mosquitos. There were two instructors on the Oxfords – F/O G. Garland and W/O E. Boucher. I quickly became friends with the latter when we discovered that at the outbreak of war we had both been working for The Gas Light and Coke Company in London, albeit in different departments. The Oxfords were sometimes used for general communications flights and whenever 'Curly', as W/O Boucher was nicknamed, was sent on any such cross-country flights, he would take me along as navigator. But Curly was not a Mosquito pilot and I had never flown in one – nor was I in a hurry to do so, as by this time the aircraft was beginning to get a bad reputation in South East Asia.

The de Havilland Mosquito had wings and fuselage of all wooden construction, covered with fabric, like many old fashioned pre-war aircraft. But more modern methods of designing the joints and securing them with state of the art casien based adhesives of great strength had resulted in a highly successful aircraft which confounded its critics when it was put into operation by the RAF. In the UK it proved to be most versatile. It was used as a twin-engined fighter, light bomber, night fighter, and for reconnaissance, particularly high level photographic reconnaissance. It was regarded as a suitable successor to the Beaufighter.

The first four Mosquitos had arrived in India in April 1943, amid some fears, even by de Havilland, that the wood and glued joints might not stand up to the high temperature and humidity, and the possibility of damage by insects such as white ants or termites, here in South East Asia. To begin with the feared problems did not materialise and Mosquitos were pressed into service, initially on 684 squadron, doing urgently needed PR work, and on 47 squadron, whose aircrews had been converted to them here at Yelahanka. However, throughout 1944 there had been several fatal crashes due to structural failures of wings, culminating in all Mosquitos being grounded for a while in November. I had heard about this while I was still on 211 Squadron. Rumours abounded as to the cause and some wags referred to the Mosquito aircraft as 'termite's delight'. However they were now flying again at Yelahanka and we assumed that the problem had been overcome. (Actually it hadn't. I only learned after the war that whilst climatic conditions and prevalence of insect attack may have been contributory causes, the problem was complex and more widespread than the powers that be admitted to the rank and file aircrew who flew in them.)

In May 1945 my former squadron was withdrawn from operational flying at Chiringa and, leaving their Beaufighters behind, the whole squadron personnel arrived here at Yelahanka for conversion to Mosquitos. They were still being led by W/C Colin Lovelock, the new CO who had taken over just as I had completed my tour, but there were many new faces and very few of the 'old guard' that I knew. However, the fact that Beaufighter squadrons were being converted made it increasingly likely that I might have to do my second tour on Mosquitos, and indeed I might even find myself back on 211 Squadron.

The war was entering a new phase. Rangoon had been re-taken and the Japanese routed from Burma, but many of the enemy troops had escaped by sea down the Malayan peninsula. They had lived to fight another day. Thus W/C Lovelock's task of getting the squadron into an operational state on Mosquitos was an urgent one. Their role would probably become more that of a strike squadron, attacking shipping and coastal targets in the Malayan Straits, as part of the taskforce which would be needed to re-take Singapore, a stronghold that the Japanese were not likely to surrender without a bloody struggle.

About a week after they had commenced training, news was received from the UK about VE day. Whilst this was a good thing for some, it had an unsettling effect on the morale of aircrews here to think that those lucky blighters back home were being stood down from operational flying. Furthermore, it seemed that most of the general public back home thought that the war was over and we in the RAF began to think of ourselves even more so as the 'forgotten air force'.

W/C Lovelock was a hard taskmaster and some thought he was driving the squadron too hard and too fast as regards their training on Mosquitos. This was to have tragic consequences for two crews.

About this time another warrant officer navigator/w named Eric (I cannot recall his surname) was posted to our unit from the UK on his 'rest' period, like myself. He had done his tour of operations in the UK on 248 Squadron, operating from bases in Cornwall. Towards the end of his tour his squadron had partly converted from Beaufighters to Mosquitos and Eric had some experience of operational flying in both. I liked Eric and we used to hang out together, discussing and comparing our completely different operational experiences. He also did much to assure me that I would soon get used to Mosquitos and he helped me begin to overcome my growing aversion to them.

I decided that I really must try to get a familiarisation flight in one and, on the 29th of June, an opportunity arose to do so. Eric and I were temporarily using the same NCOs mess as the 211 squadron aircrews and after lunch we sat in the lounge area drinking coffee. Neither of us had any duties that afternoon and we had already decided that we would take a long walk back, right round the perimeter of the airfield, to our unit flight office instead getting on the truck. Some 211 aircrew came and sat opposite and I was surprised to see Joe Smith, a navigator whom I had not seen since we had been together on No.32 OTU at Patricia Bay in Canada. It seemed that Joe had done some operational flying but then his pilot had been killed in an accident. I cannot remember where this had been but he had then been shunted about a bit and was now crewed up with another pilot and had been posted to 211 squadron to complete a tour on Mosquitos.

After about ten minutes the transport truck arrived and Joe said he would have to go as he was flying this afternoon. I had already told him that I had never flown in a Mosquito and I then took the opportunity of asking him whether he could fix it for me to get a flight in one sometime.

I was taken aback when he replied, "Sure, how about this afternoon?" We and three other crews are doing a fighter affiliation exercise with some Spitfires from No.4 Squadron RIAF. It will only be local flying. Shall I go and ask my pilot if you can go up instead of me?" I had to make a quick decision. In my mind I still had this aversion – fear almost – of Mosquitos, but this was just the opportunity that I needed.

"OK, that would be fine," I said. As he got up to leave the table I added as an afterthought, "What's your pilot's name?"

"Geoff Lowcock," he replied.

I felt stunned. My mind flew back to the several hours I had spent talking to Geoff Lowcock, sitting on that grassy mound outside Comilla station, and that strange feeling of foreboding I had had about him. I now had what I can only describe as an overpowering premonition. I did not actually foresee the crash, but a little voice from deep within myself insisted 'On no account must you fly with Geoff Lowcock.'

Quickly, I half rose to my feet and, feeling rather stupid and very embarrassed, called out after Joe, who had just left the table, "Oh, Joe, I've just remembered that I can't fly this afternoon, there is something I have to do."

"OK," he replied, "some other time perhaps." Then he and most of the 211 crowd left the mess to get on the transport to the airfield, leaving Eric and I sitting at the table. We were in no hurry to leave.

Eric had said nothing during my conversation with Joe but I did notice that he had given me a funny look when I said that I had 'something else to do', because he knew perfectly well that I hadn't. He now asked me why I had 'changed my mind' as he put it, but in a manner that seemed to imply that he thought I had 'chickened out', as indeed I had – for no rational reason. I felt I could not explain to him about my 'premonition' regarding Lowcock and made some feeble excuse that I did not feel like flying that afternoon.

After a while we left the mess, went a few hundred yards along the road and began our walk along the edge of the airfield as we had planned. It was not a bad day, not too hot. There was very little cloud about but the sky was hazy. At around 1430 hours we saw four Mosquitos take off. About ten minutes later they came back over the airfield, cruising at about 3,000 feet, neatly formed up in a diamond formation, heading in the direction of Bangalore, presumably to their rendezvous with the fighters. Eric and I walked on, chatting. He came from Birmingham and had a 'brummie' accent, which tended to become more pronounced when he was excited. After several more minutes he suddenly grabbed my arm and shouted agitatedly, "Look! There's a Mozzie going in!" I turned my head and saw, about three miles distant, a Mosquito plummeting absolutely vertically downwards into the ground. At that instant it was about 300 feet from disaster but I knew that the crew were already doomed – there could be no escape. I also knew with *unquestionable certainty* that the pilot was Lowcock. The actual impact was obscured by distant treetops but we saw an enormous ball of orange flame and black smoke billow upwards. I had just witnessed a fatal crash but all I felt was a great sense of calm and relief that I had not been on that plane. Eric, on the other hand was still quite agitated.

"Let's hurry up and get to the flight office and find out who it was," he said.

"It's Lowcock," I replied. "How can you know that? It could be any one of the four," he said. It was not the time to start talking about paranormal cognition so I replied quietly, "I just *know*".

We were not allowed to cross the runway and so we had to continue walking right to the end and back up the other side, and it was about forty minutes before we got to the flight office. Lots of people were milling about and we began to piece together what had happened. It had indeed been W/O Lowcock who had been flying at the rear of the formation when he was jumped by two Spitfires. In attempting to take evasive action he must have stalled the Mosquito and dived straight into the ground. I learned that Joe had not been with him. Another pilot, F/Sgt W. Wilkes, had been in the navigator's seat.

Tragically, the aircraft had fallen into the middle of the small village of Kogilu, where some form of religious festival was taking place. It must have been a horrific sight for those in the RAF ambulance and crash tender first at the scene. A few medics with first aid kits and a handful of morphine ampoules were faced with scores of injured and badly burned civilians, including many women and children, needing urgent medical attention. Likewise, a crash tender crew with a foam extinguishers capable of dealing with an aircraft fire were faced with a bamboo village blazing virtually from end to end. Others had rushed to the site to do what they could but urgent calls had to be made to Bangalore's civilian emergency services to send ambulances, fire engines and police. It was a major incident.

The final death toll at Kogilu was 38 villagers killed and nearly 100 injured. For the next few days the whole squadron was in shock, but I did not get much of a chance to talk to any of them.

This was a black day for 211 Squadron, but worse was to follow. A few days later on 2nd of July the CO had arranged for a little air display before some invited guests from the Southern Army Command HQ in Bangalore, together with a few civilian dignitaries from the city. In view of the tragedy at Koligu, many were surprised that W/C Lovelock allowed this to proceed, but he did. I was not involved, but was just a bystander watching from the side of the airfield, close to the control tower building where the guests were assembled. It was not a good day, the sky was overcast and the cloud base was rather low. Two minor mishaps occurred.

To begin with, three Mosquitos were to take-off in a tight V formation, with their wingtips linked by brightly coloured bunting. The runway was just wide enough to allow this, but in the event the aircraft on the right-hand side swung slightly. The pilot recovered and got airborne safely, but had moved to the right sufficiently to break the bunting. This spoiled the whole effect, particularly when they subsequently did a low-level pass along the length of the runway, still in tight formation but with one length of bunting trailing rather pathetically in the slipstream.

A bit later, another Mosquito flew along the runway to demonstrate precision bombing by dropping a flour-sack 'bomb' onto a small circular target marked on the ground. But the pilot misjudged it and the 'bomb' hit and damaged the wing of a Thunderbolt aircraft which was parked near the edge of the runway.

But it was during the finale that the tragedy occurred.

Six Mosquitos, led by W/C Lovelock, were to fly across at right angles to the runway, approaching from behind the control tower building. Each aircraft in turn would make a shallow dive-bombing attack, dropping a small, 10-pound practice bomb on an old, derelict aircraft positioned about 300 yards beyond the opposite side of the runway, in full view of the spectators on the building. I watched the aircraft approaching and thought they would have to abort the demonstration as the cloud base was so low. Of course, I could not hear what was being said over the RT, but it seemed that the order to make the attack was left until the last minute. The leader made his attack and hit the target spot on, but to me, as an onlooker, it appeared that the following aircraft were too low to make their dives safely. In the event, one of them misjudged it and 'mushed' into the ground. The Pilot, W/O K. Webster and his navigator F/Sgt. J. Hopes were killed instantly as the Mosquito shattered into pieces, although, quite remarkably, without any fire.

This horrific crash occurred in full view of the spectators, but just far enough away so that no one was injured by the flying debris.

This was an even blacker day for 211 Squadron, and I was saddened by it all.

For the next couple of days the Squadron was in turmoil. I understand that recriminations and mutterings of criticisms of W/C Lovelock abounded but I was out of it because I went away on a two-day trip in an Oxford with one of the 1672 MCU pilots. When we got back most of the 211 crews had flown off to Madras in the Mosquitos allocated to them, where they were to continue practice flying as a squadron.

Towards the end of the month we, as 1672 MCU, were to be moved to Ranchi in Bihar, and three remaining Mosquitos were to be flown there. F/O Garland was to lead the formation of three and he asked me to be his navigator. I had flown with him before in Oxfords and thought that he was a good pilot. Strangely, my qualms about the aircraft seemed to be fading and I was finally about to get my first flight in one. Thus, on the 9th August, we took off in Mosquito RF.543, accompanied by the other two, for a 3 hour 50 minute flight to Ranchi. It was not, of course, at low-level; we flew at about 5000 feet. The weather was good and the flight was long enough for me to get used to the unfamiliar cockpit. The other two pilots were also instructors and, to make our arrival a bit spectacular, F/O Garland got permission from Ranchi to do a 'Prince of Wales Feather' manoeuvre over the airfield.

As we approached we did a long shallow dive, arriving over the airfield at about 1000 feet and maximum speed. When F/O Garland gave the order to 'break' he pulled back on the control column and up we went in the steepest climb and highest 'G' forced I had yet experienced. The others banked to right and left and it must have looked quite impressive from the ground. (Many years later, after the war, I read an account of the problems of construction and quality control on the wings of wartime Mosquitos. Apparently, none of the aircraft in India at the time, including RF 543, could be guaranteed not to have this problem. And if any aerobatic manoeuvre was likely to lead to structural failure of a wing, surely it would be the one we had just done!)

For the first few days at Ranchi nobody knew what the future programme of the unit would be but, as far as I was concerned, I was reconciled to the fact that within a week or two I would be posted to an operation squadron to do a second tour, almost certainly on Mosquitos. Now that I had flown in one I thought that maybe they were not so bad.

But it was not to be. Within a few days we heard the completely unexpected news about the atom bombs dropped on Japan. Then, on 15th August, VJ Day was announced. This, of course, meant that I would not have to do a second tour after all. Gin flowed that day!

5.   Mandalay

Prequel

From the age of about six, I became more and more aware of the Great War, as the First World War was then referred to, from hearing my parents and teachers talk about it and from the many adventure stories in comic books which I began to read. It seemed to me to be something that had happened long, long ago but in fact it had ended only sixteen months before I was born. As I grew a bit older and was taken on trips to the cinema I became fascinated by some of the early war films. Those which featured warplanes such as 'Hell's Angels', 'Dawn Patrol', and 'Wings', made a very great impression on me.

At that time I had only one close friend, a boy of my own age called Dickie. He lived opposite me and shared my fascination with matters relating to the Royal Flying Corps, as it was known in those days. I used to spend a lot of time in his garden, where, although we had some other common interests such as Hornby trains and Meccano, we more often than not finished up playing war games. In a disused conservatory he had several old tea chests, sheets, chairs, planks and other items suitable for building pretend warplanes in which we spent many hours imitating the exploits of our film heroes.

Dickie, who was more extrovert than me, generally appointed himself as the pilot, while I took on the role of the observer. I sat in the rear cockpit, actually a tea chest, locating enemy positions on a map and dropping bombs over the side, just as we had seen in the films. Dickie would get into dog fights with German fighters and shoot them down whilst I would stand up in my cockpit and fire my machine gun, made out of a bit of wood, at enemy planes sneaking up on us from the rear, or at anti-aircraft gunners that I spotted on the ground. The garden rang with the 'rat-a-tat-tat-tat-tat-

tat' sounds of simulated machine gunfire. Countless times we saved each other's lives in the face of the wicked enemy.

Little did I know then that, in the space of around ten years, war would come again and we would experience playing these roles for real, albeit separately and in different theatres of war.

As we got older we grew out of these games but also we tended to grow apart. He went to Woodford High School, a private school, where he mixed with friends in a higher social group. I went to Churchfields Council Boy's School and then, at the age of thirteen, to Leyton Technical College, to study engineering. We therefore had different friends and developed different interests. At that time the outbreak of the Spanish Civil War tended to polarise people's political views and I found, from occasional chats with Dickie, that we had drifted apart in this respect also. He had leanings towards fascism, no doubt influenced by the then widespread propaganda of Oswald Moseley. On the other hand, I favoured communism, influenced by some young radicals, mostly Graduates from Oxford, with whom I rubbed shoulders in the laboratories at Watson House, where I had started work.

Shortly after the outbreak of the Second World War we moved to Greenford because both my father and I were working on the west side of London and commuting daily across the city was becoming more difficult. As a result, I lost contact with Dickie.

During the early days of the war my work at Watson House was classified as a 'reserved occupation' and I was not called up. However, by the summer of 1941 it became obvious that the war was going to continue for some time and growing feelings of patriotism led me to volunteer for service in the RAF as an Air Navigator. I was immediately accepted but was put on six months deferred service. On entry I found that I was earmarked for training as a 'Navigator/W', which was the equivalent of the former 'Observer' because it involved additional instruction in Wireless Operation, Air Gunnery, Air Photography and Reconnaissance.

By the end of September 1942 I qualified as a Wireless Operator at No.1 Signals School Cranwell and had just been told that I, together with three of my pals, would be going overseas for my navigation training. I was feeling quite excited about it when at that moment I received a letter from my father which contained some news that stunned and saddened me. He had heard from our old neighbour at Woodford that Dickie, who unbeknown to me must have joined the RAF quite early on and become a fighter pilot, had been shot down over the English channel and reported 'missing believed killed'. This news brought home to me the reality of war and I took a while to come to terms with it. I tried to imagine what it had been like for him. Had some German fighter sneaked up on him from the rear? Quite irrationally I felt that I had let him down in some way by not having been there, and that maybe I would avenge his death once I started operational flying navigating bombers over Germany.

However, the dictates of the war caused my career in the RAF to take a completely different course from that which I had envisaged. I finished up doing my operational flying in two-man crewed Beaufighters, where I really did have to carry out all the duties of an Observer. I was posted to a squadron in South East Asia where, only seven days after arrival, I found myself on an operational sortie, during which I felt that Dickie had been avenged. For the first time, and as it happens the only time, I fired a gun in anger. It was not German soldiers who paid the price but four or five hapless Japanese gunners, but to me, at that moment, they were all the same – the 'wicked enemy'. The following story is about that trip and that moment.

Because my pilot, P/O Geoff Vardigans, had been detained in hospital in Allahabad, I had been instructed to travel on by myself to join No.211 Squadron. By a stroke of luck I managed to cadge a lift in a Dakota to Calcutta, but the last part of the journey to Comilla, by rail then river steamer and then rail again, had been very wearisome. Finally, after a six mile ride in the back of a three ton truck along an extremely bumpy road, I arrived at my first operational RAF station.

It was absolutely nothing like I had pictured. Indeed it was about the nearest you could get to a World War One airfield 'somewhere in France'. The airfield was just that, a field with a bedraggled windsock in one corner. Beaufighters were dispersed around, under trees, with no protecting earthworks. There were no shelters and not a sandbag in sight, in fact, the airfield was undefended except for sentries posted at night. The flight offices were in tents. Another small tent at one side of the field served as 'flying control' and was manned by a 'duty pilot' whose only contact with aircraft taking off or landing was by an Aldis signal lamp. There was no equipment to make R/T contact with aircraft.

Virtually all the buildings comprising the station were of bamboo construction, known as Bashas. There was no running water and lighting was by hurricane lamps, except in a few buildings such as the Cook House and the three small Mess rooms. These were lit by electricity from a small generator, which failed frequently. Apart from a few local workers, bearers, *pani-wallahs* and *char-wallahs* the only personnel on the station were members of the squadron.

It was a close-knit community, where relations between officers, NCOs and airmen were relatively informal. I was found a bed in a hut, which I shared with two Flight Sergeants – 'Tubby' Tompson and his navigator 'China' Whale – who later became close friends of mine.

When I sought out the acting Navigation Officer to get some maps I found that he was P/O 'Sammy' Parker, whom I already knew from Crosby-on-Eden. He had done several trips and was able to give me some advice.

"Best forget most of what we were taught at navigation school," he said with a laugh. "Most of the trips are at low-level, with your pilot frequently taking evasive action. It is not practical to use charts for plotting, or to use the normal navigators log form, and in any case we don't have any charts or log forms."

"So you don't try to keep an air plot going then?" I said.

"Goodness no!" he replied. "Most of the time you will be track-crawling. Plot tracks and make measurements on topographical maps and use a knee pad for jotting down times and other observations."

The RAF manual on 'Air Navigation' devoted only one quarter of a page to 'Low-Flying Navigation Over the Land', and this mainly about what navigational procedures are *not* practical. I had already realised that it was an art that must be learned by experience, but we had not done any low flying over land during our training.

So here I was, about to get some experience and learn – but over *enemy* territory! Then, to make matters worse, he handed me a set of maps of Burma, with a warning that some of them were 'not very reliable'. When I studied them later, I found that the maps, which were 1:1,000,000 scale, were based on ancient surveys, some as long ago as 1914. Hardly the best aid, I thought, for map reading over a country where rivers can change their course over a period of time and where the appearance of the landscape can alter considerably with the seasons. Lush green valleys may become dried-up riverbeds with parched brown countryside in a short space of time.

I learned that Geoff and I had been assigned to 'B' flight and the morning after my arrival I duly reported to the Officer I/C at his tent. He welcomed me but said that there was nothing for me to do until Geoff arrived. He suggested that I hang around and talk to other navigators to pick up some tips. He then added, hesitantly, "Actually, there is a P/O Moffat in 'A' flight who is without a navigator at the moment and he has asked me whether you would be prepared to fly with him. I have said that it is entirely up to you. It would only be temporarily, because P/O Vardigans and yourself have definitely been allocated to me and you will be flying with him as soon as he arrives.

Already somewhat bemused by the strangeness of the whole environment, I was taken aback at the thought of flying with someone else and my first reaction was to say no, and to wait for Geoff. However, I said that I would go and see F/O Moffat.

On the way I bumped into Sammy again, who gave me a brief run-down on 'Moff', as everyone apparently called him.

"Ah," he said. "You mean the 'mad' Canadian. He's a good pilot but a bit of a 'know-all'. His navigator got shot in the foot recently and has been sent to Comilla. Moff is keen to get flying again but the CO won't let him fly without a navigator, even though he says he is good at map reading and is getting to know Burma 'like the back of his hand'. The word 'mad' did not worry me, as it was an epithet frequently applied to Canadians in the RAF. This was mainly because they tended to lack discipline on the ground. However, Sammy's remark about map-reading made me think that it might not be such a bad idea for me to fly with him. It would enable me to get some experience before Geoff came, but with a pilot who would not be relying too much on me alone. Accordingly, I sought out Moff and, after a short conversation, volunteered to fly with him.

Thus it came about that one afternoon, only six days after joining the squadron, Moff and I, together with five other crews, were briefed for a trip the following morning. It was to be an attack with rocket projectiles on the railway marshalling yard in the town of Mandalay. I did not realise at the time that this strike, by six Beaufighters against a specific target such as this, was untypical of the work the squadron did. Normally one, or occasionally two, aircraft would be sent to carry out offensive patrols along selected stretches of road, railway or river, deep within enemy-held territory, to deter them from using them during daylight hours.

Mandalay was situated wholly on the east bank of the Irrawaddy, river which was just over a mile wide at that point. We planned to cross the river about three miles north of the town, where we would soon pass over a railway, which ran out through the northern suburbs. Making a sharp turn right and following this branch line south would lead us directly to the yard, which we would be approaching from the 'back', or buffer stop end of the sidings. By this time, all six aircraft would be spaced out in line astern, still flying at rooftop height, and it would only be necessary for each aircraft in turn to climb up two or three hundred feet in order to aim and fire a salvo of rockets. Each pilot was allocated a specific target. The leading aircraft would fly the length of the yard to the 'neck' or entrance where there was a concentrated arrangement of points and a large signal cabin from which all the switching was done. The following pilots were allocated targets such as the engine sheds, coal stacks, water tower, turntable, etc, located progressively nearer the back end. This way, each pilot would get a good view of his target without it being obscured by smoke and debris from the explosion of the one in front.

The attack was timed to take place at about 0900 hours, which worried me slightly. Surely, I thought, the ack-ack gun crews were more likely to be fresh on duty and more alert at this hour? But what worried me more was that apparently Moff was the senior of the pilots and would be the leader. Did this mean that I, the inexperienced new navigator, would be responsible for getting them there? As we left the briefing room I expressed my concern to Moff, who said, "Don't you worry about map reading. I'll get them there. All I want you to do is to keep a sharp look out for fighters."

The following morning, the 25th of April, we all climbed aboard our aircraft. Moff and I were in Beaufighter NE292. It was quite a hassle for the ground staff, with their limited equipment, to get as many as six Beaufighters started at the same time. Eventually, when we had all taxied to one end of the field, Moff took off first at 0730 hours and did a very wide left hand circuit so that the others could make successively tighter turns and form up behind us. I watched them from the air, taking off one by one and about seven minutes later we turned on to a heading of 112°, on course for Mandalay, with the other five behind us in a loose echelon port formation. We were on our way.

It was a fine morning, with blue sky above, but we could see quite a lot of cumulus cloud ahead, over the foothills of the mountains which we were going to cross. We were climbing steadily, but the hills were getting higher also. After about 25 minutes we were at 4,000 feet, but the forested hilltops were still only about 1,000 feet below. We were now just below the base of the clouds and we would have to get above them. Rather than look for a gap, Moff decided to stay on track and climb up through them. After about five minutes in cloud we broke through into clear air with blue sky again.

Moff asked me to let him know when all five had emerged. I was fascinated watching them pop up one by one out of a sea of fluffy white cloud into the sunshine. They now began to close up a bit. I had never flown in formation with more than two other Beaufighters before and it was an impressive sight to see five of them behind us, starkly contrasted against the white background. How I wished that I had a camera.

We climbed on steadily to about 9,000 feet. When the clouds below started to break up and I got a good view of the Chin Hills, where some of the peaks were still barely a 1,000 feet below us. By 0825 we had reached the Myittha valley at a point where I could see that we were on track. On the other side of the valley the hills got progressively lower and we started to lose height. After 15 minutes we were down to the central plain and flying really low at about 50 feet. We were now approaching the Chindwin river, which we would cross at a point about 16 miles north of the town of Monywa, where there were known to be two landing strips. It was important to keep a sharp lookout for fighters in this area but at the same time I was trying to practise my low-level map reading. As we crossed the Chindwin it seemed to me that we were about three miles south of our intended track, but I said nothing to Moff.

As we swept on the terrain became more featureless. Roads were little more than tracks and there were stretches of marshland. I felt that we were drifting too far south but I couldn't be sure. I was still hesitant about saying anything to Moff that might make him think I was being critical, after all, he was an officer and at that time I was only a sergeant. Then we passed over the Shwebo road and I was now sure that we had crossed it five miles south of where we should have. If we stayed on this course we would cross the river and arrive too near the centre of Mandalay to use the branch line as a 'lead in' as we had planned. This could lead to chaos as aircraft might get in each other's way if they had to individually locate the target and attack from a different direction than that planned.

I was now so worried that I told Moff that I thought we were off course. He almost snapped back at me that he knew where he was and that I should be keeping a look out, not trying to map read. I think in fact that he had already realised he needed to alter course but at that moment, much to his chagrin, there was a crackle on the R/T and a terse, "You're too far south Moff," from one of the other pilots. Moff acknowledged it with an even more terse, "I know," and altered course a few degrees to port. Obviously the others were so concerned that one of them had risked breaking R/T silence to warn Moff. Secretly, I felt pleased that this had happened, but I also felt concerned that the other navigators might be thinking that I was to blame.

Five minutes later we reached the Irrawaddy, at the place where we had intended to cross. It was a mass of sandbanks interspersed with water channels and it took us nearly a minute to skim across it, flying just a few feet above the water. I was still facing backwards and it was an impressive sight to see the others, now in line astern and spaced out more in preparation for the attack, strung out behind us over the river.

When we reached the other bank there was no opposition from machine gun fire, and almost immediately we were over what was obviously a residential area. There were bungalows and chalets, some very picturesque, with narrow, tree-lined lanes between. Many had gardens with little lawns, surrounded by leafy shrubs and hedges, which no doubt made them secluded on the ground but not so from the air. I saw a few people about, who jumped and looked up startled after we, the leading aircraft, had streaked over them. This was a clear testimonial to the truth of the legendary reputation of the Beaufighter for its quietness when low flying, a reputation that had earned it the sobriquet *Whispering Death*. I felt I wanted to call out to these people that we had not come to harm them, and to apologise for intruding on the privacy of their little gardens.

We got to the railway and as we flashed over it I saw that there was a narrow road running along on the other side of it. A small grass bank and a fence, made out of old railway sleepers, separated the road from the railway. Walking along the road by the grass bank was a boy, probably about twelve years old. He was dressed in a grubby pair of khaki shorts with a white short-sleeved shirt, worn outside the shorts and flapping about. He wasn't carrying anything but was walking, barefoot, in a happy go lucky manner in the direction of the town centre. The first thing he must have heard was a tremendous *whoosh* as ten tons of Beaufighter, travelling at 300 feet per second, passed about 30 feet over his head. He must have been in my vision for little more than two or three seconds but during this time I witnessed changes in his demeanour that almost seemed to be in slow motion. At first he didn't change his gait but looked up, startled. Then he quickened his pace. He was looking directly at me and I saw his eyes open wide with fear as he comprehended what was happening. He ducked and crouched in the road. Again, all this was after we had crossed the road, otherwise I could not have seen it. By this time Moff had started to bank steeply to the right, so I could still see the boy. I could now see the second aircraft about to cross at almost the same spot. Maybe the boy heard this one coming, because he jumped up and ran, panic stricken, to the other side of the road where there were some bushes. I then lost sight of him but he must have crouched there, terrified, as five more Beaufighters flashed over him in quick succession.

I felt a great wave of compassion, not just for this boy but for the other civilians I was seeing, going about their business on this lovely sunny morning. Also I felt relieved, because this meant that up to this moment there had obviously not been any general air raid warning. We had apparently achieved complete surprise and were over the town, only about a minute away from our target, without the slightest sign of any opposition.

By now Moff had swung round and was flying south down the railway line. As I swivelled my seat round to face forward for the attack I saw Fort Dufferin on a high point where the land sloped upwards off to our left. We had been told that there were some British prisoners of war kept there. I could see a row of narrow windows in the wall facing us and if anyone had been looking out they would certainly see us. What would they be feeling, I wondered? Of course, there would also be Japanese military personnel and no doubt telephones were frantically being picked up there and at any other observation posts on this side of town. But they were too late. We were only half a minute away from our target.

"This is it," said Moff, as he climbed up sharply. Then he put the nose down into a shallow dive and I got a good but brief look at the yard. I knew the layout from the photographs we had studied at briefing. There was a fair amount of rolling stock but not a locomotive in sight. Along the top of the fuselage I could now see the large signal box in front of us as Moff aimed the aircraft, using his reflector sight. Then he fired – all eight rockets in one salvo. I checked that all eight had left the aircraft and saw them streak down and hit the target spot-on. There was a huge explosion and a column of flame, smoke and debris shot into the air. Then I lost sight of it as Moff pulled out with a violent turn and bank to the right.

It had been agreed that aircraft would break away to the right and to the left alternately. Those turning left would fly eastwards out of the town, then circle right round northwards, crossing back over the river well to the north. Moff, and aircraft Nos 3 and 5 would turn right and head directly westwards across the town to the waterfront, then across the river, where we would set course for base and hopefully merge with the other three so that we would be in formation again by the time we got near to Monywa.

It would only take us about a minute to reach the river and, as we sped over the rooftops, I turned round to face backwards again. We were now over a busier part of town and I was surprised to see people, cyclists and even one or two commercial vehicles still moving about, apparently normally. Even if there had not been any public air raid warning, surely they would have heard the explosions from the goods yard? But at that moment I saw two ack-ack shells burst in the sky far over on the eastern side of the town. These were far too high to be any threat to the Beaufighters leaving in that direction, but at least it indicated that at last someone in the enemy's air defence system had woken up.

We were now approaching the waterfront, where there might be some machine gun posts and, as a precaution, Moff had started weaving. I had my rear gun unhooked and ready to return fire if necessary. We were over commercial buildings and warehouses, only seconds away from the water's edge when suddenly I saw them. Five Japanese soldiers had come running out of a door near the top of a three-storey building onto a flat-roofed extension at one end. The roof had a brick parapet round it and in one corner was a gun in a sandbagged emplacement. It was a rapid firing ack-ack gun of the Bofors type, a weapon far more deadly to an aircraft than a machine gun. If they got to the gun and aimed it at our Beaufighter as we retreated across the open water they could hardly fail to hit us from their high vantage point. They had to be stopped.

We were banking to the right at that moment and by chance my gun was pointing almost directly at them. Already high on adrenalin I experienced a sudden change in consciousness as I seemed to realise for the first time that this really was war. It was kill or be killed. I felt intense anger and hatred for these men as I pulled the trigger and opened fire.

It was probably the 'rat-a-tat-tat' sound of my gun that caused thoughts of Dickie and the war games we played in his garden at Woodford to come flooding into my mind. For a moment I had a mental flashback. It was not Moff who was flying the aircraft but Dickie, and I was in a tea chest firing a wooden gun at the wicked enemy who were trying to kill him.

But the bullets I saw spattering across the flat roof below were real. The men went sprawling in all directions, but before I could be certain that nobody would reach the gun the aircraft starting to roll over as Moff began to bank violently to the left. The scene was snatched from my view and all I could see in my gunsight was blue sky as my gun was now pointing uselessly up in the air. Although I was still holding it, the gravitational force took me by surprise and I could not stop the gun being flung right over to the other side. I was now looking down on the left hand side of the aircraft and saw that we were just passing over the last row of buildings alongside the wharf. I saw bullets spraying across the corrugated iron roof of one, then across a backstreet and onto the roof of another. For a moment I thought that someone else was firing, but then I realised it was me. Everything had happened so quickly, and I had been so desperate to stop any of those soldiers getting to the gun, that I had forgotten to take my finger off the trigger.

We levelled up as we swooped down over the wharf and headed out across the river, just a few feet above the water. I was trying to keep my eyes on the position where I knew the gun to be, because during those dramatic few seconds I had also seen Beaufighter No.3 in the distance, following us out over the rooftops. Sammy and his pilot Steve were in this aircraft. They were slightly further south than us and would present a better, side-on, target for that ack-ack gun if there was anybody to man it. I wanted to ask Moff to shout a warning to them over the R/T, but he started to speak to me over the intercom, wasting valuable seconds.

"That was you firing wasn't it?" he said accusingly. "You frightened the life out of me. I thought that someone was firing at us. You should tell me if you are going to open fire."

I explained to him about the Bofors gun, which he had not seen, and that I had had to make a split-second decision to fire. There had simply been no time to speak to him.

By now we were moving rapidly out of range and there was no sign of firing from that gun, or indeed from anywhere else along the wharf. Moments later, I was relieved to see aircraft No.3 sweeping safely out across the water, unopposed. By the time we had reached the other bank I was also able to report to Moff that I could now see aircraft No.5 following a long way behind us, but apparently OK. Slowly, they caught up with us and then, after about ten minutes, Moff became anxious about aircraft Nos 2, 4 and 6, which were still nowhere in sight.

I was looking out on the starboard side, where they should have been visible by now. It is surprisingly difficult to see other low-flying aircraft, even if they are only a mile or so away, and it was another five minutes before I suddenly spotted them, flying together. The two groups gradually merged and by the time we crossed the road and railway north of Monywa we were flying in our original formation again. A few minutes later we came to the last danger spot, the Chindwin river. Although this was only a quarter of a mile wide, and we crossed it at a 'quiet' point where there were no marked ferry crossings or villages, there was always the risk of coming under fire from some of the numerous machine gun posts the Japanese had deployed along its banks. But we all crossed it without incident and soon we started the long climb up to the comparative safety of the Chin Hills.

Over the mountains the weather was still fine, we were on our way home, and we could relax a bit. But my mind was still in a whirl as I tried to analyse the kaleidoscopic thoughts and emotions I had experienced over Mandalay. I had felt deep compassion, an emotion virtually unknown to me before, exhilaration, then real anger and intense hatred all within the space of a few minutes. For me this was the day the war had really started.

We arrived back over the field at Bhatpara, still in formation. Most of the personnel on the squadron would have seen us leave together earlier that morning and they must have been thrilled to see all six Beaufighters return safely. Moff and I were first to land, at 1050 hours, having been airborne for 3 hours 20 minutes. At the de-briefing there were congratulations all round. Our low flying tactics had taken the enemy's air defences of the second largest town in Burma completely by surprise. In the space of about one minute we had delivered the equivalent of 48 high-explosive artillery shells on an important link in their railway system, with devastating results.

Not one aircraft had been lost, but I don't think that Moff ever stopped to think what might have happened if he had been flying without an Observer, as he had wanted to. Coming back across the Irrawaddy, like Dickie, the first he might have known about that gun would have been a deadly hail of 30mm cannon shells, capable of penetrating armour plate and aluminium alike, ploughing into the rear of his aircraft.

Observers do have their uses!

6.   Scramble!

During the Battle of Britain in 1940, most people were made familiar, through the medium of newsreels or films, with the image of fighter pilots dressed at the ready in blue battledress, flying boots and Mae West life jackets, sitting about outside their flight office, trying hard to relax, each doing his own thing, be it playing cards, reading, writing a scribbled note home, playing with the dog or just fooling around, but each knowing in the back of his mind that the adrenalin-raising bell might ring at any moment, signalling 'scramble for take-off'!

What must it be like? – I used to think. That rush to the plane, the ground crew getting the engine started in double quick time, hurriedly taxiing out and taking off, often not knowing where you were going until you were airborne and received RT instructions as to what course to fly and what height to fly to intercept some enemy aircraft.

But later, when I volunteered to join the RAF as aircrew, I was selected as a navigator/wireless operator, not a pilot. After extensive training I became one of a two-man crew on Beaufighters with Geoff as my pilot. We finally started operational flying on 211 Squadron at Bhatpara in East Bengal. The role of the squadron at this time was that of interdiction. This involved long range low-level sorties deep into Japanese-held territory over Burma.

The system here was that a despatch rider from nearby 169 Wing headquarters would arrive about midday with a 'Form B', which would detail the orders for next day's operations. Bhatpara was only a small grass landing field, it did not have equipment for direct W/T communications, and the telephone system was not secure enough. Usually one or two aircraft from each of 'A' and 'B' flights would be required and targets – generally selected stretches of road, rail or river – would be specified. Sometimes aircraft would go in pairs but mostly single aircraft would go to different targets at different times. The details on the form 'B' would first be studied by the CO, the Intelligence Officer and the two Flight Commanders. The latter would pass instructions to the ground crews as to how many aircraft were to be made ready and whether they were to be additionally armed with RPs (Rocket Projectiles). The Flight Commanders would instruct the crews in their respective flights to attend in the briefing room at an agreed time, usually in the late afternoon. In each flight, the crews flew in rotation and so Geoff and I knew in advance when it would be our turn to be briefed for a sortie the following day.

Thus 'scrambled' (hurried or unscheduled) take-offs did not happen on our squadron ... or so I thought ... until one day, the 13th of May, when the normal pattern of events was broken and I had an experience similar to that of Battle of Britain fighter pilots.

We had flown an operational sortie the day before and so today was a rest day. Rest days were precious. We seldom had any other duties to perform and could really relax in the knowledge that we would probably not be flying the following day either, although no doubt we would be briefed in the afternoon for a sortie on the subsequent day.

Just after lunch, I was sitting outside our Basha, where there was a bit of shade, and had started to read a book, but it was hot and sunny and I began to doze off. Suddenly I was aroused by the sound of a jeep approaching along the rough track, being driven fast enough to make the dust swirl. It was unusual for any vehicle to use this track because it didn't lead anywhere else, and I felt a slight sense of foreboding – something was up. This feeling changed more to alarm as I saw that not only was Geoff driving it but also he was dressed in operational flying kit. Without getting out of the jeep, and as he proceeded to turn it around, he called out, "Get ready for flying right away Denny! I'm going to pick up Steve and Sammy and will be back for you in ten minutes."

"OK…" I said. "But where are we going?"

"Don't know yet!" he shouted, as he drove away.

It was panic stations. I had been wearing just a pair of khaki shorts. Now, in the heat of early afternoon, I had to quickly find a singlet and briefs and then don that heavy one-piece Beedon suit. I say 'heavy' because, although the overall itself was not heavy, it had many pockets, crammed with items of kit for jungle survival. It seemed to take ages to get my thick socks and marching boots on and laced up (we normally wore these instead of the normal flying boots for operations over Burma). Then I fitted my webbing belt, checking that my revolver was secure in its holster, lanyard around my neck and that ammunition pouches, dagger, water bottle, etc, were all correctly attached. Then I put on my Mae West lifejacket and lastly, on top of everything, I put on my parachute harness.

Already perspiring from the heat and exertion, I attempted to sit on my bed. I say 'attempted' because the rectangular pack containing my inflatable dinghy was attached to the bottom rear of my harness, making sitting down difficult. Aboard the aircraft, of course, the dinghy pack fitted into the navigator's 'bucket' seat, forming a cushion, on which you sat (although 'cushion' is not the word navigators would use to describe it after the first three or four hours of a trip!). The Navigator's parachute clipped onto the front of his harness but was normally carried loose and stowed beside him in the aircraft.

I was, of course, familiar with the drill of putting on this flying gear, but on the eight trips I had done to date this had been done in a more leisurely manner, in the relative cool of early morning, for take-offs usually before 0800 hours. This was the first time I had had to do it in a hurry, in the hottest part of the day, and I didn't like it.

During this commotion of getting ready, my hut mates Tubby and China had been, and still were, lying on their beds, muttering sympathetic noises, although at one point I do remember Tubby saying something like, "I wonder what's up? Must be something big, like an attack on an airstrip maybe..." which was not really the sort of speculation I wanted to hear.

I was still wondering if there was anything I had forgotten when Geoff came back with Steve and Sammy. I clambered on to the jeep and Geoff drove quickly the short distance to the field, where two Beaufighters were ready with ground crews standing by. S/L Muller-Rowlands, the O/C of 'B' Flight, was also by the aircraft and told us to fly to Chittagong, where we would be briefed. Even he did not know where we would be going. Geoff and I were in NE.298 V and Steve and Sammy in LZ.479 O. I did not know at the time that both these aircraft had been flown by other crews earlier this same day on pre-dawn take-offs, arriving back at 0730 hours. Fortunately, they had not suffered any damage but the ground crews had only just finished servicing them.

We climbed aboard, the engines were started and run up in double quick time and we taxied, or maybe 'trundled' is a better description, over the rough grass to one end of the field. Steve took off first and we followed about half a minute later at 1336 hours. It would take about half an hour to reach Chittagong, so we only climbed to around 2,000 feet, keeping below a few scattered cumulus clouds that were already starting to build up, as they usually did in the afternoons in this pre-monsoon period. Our track converged towards the coastline, which had a railway line running parallel to it, leading directly to Chittagong. Geoff was following Steve and both were following the line of the railway, so I had little to do except worry – which I was good at when I had little to do.

Thoughts drifted into my mind... *Water bottle!* I had not filled it with fresh water. Following a more normal afternoon briefing I would refill it in the Mess (the only source of safe chlorinated water) during the evening meal, ready for an early morning take-off. But this sortie had been at short notice in the afternoon and I had not thought about it. I remembered that I had drunk from it during the morning and knew it was not full. Then *Maps!* In my navigation bag I had four maps that covered the whole area of Burma over which we normally flew. But I had originally been issued with two further maps of the more northern areas where Geoff and I had not hitherto been. I did not normally keep these in my navigation bag and in the rush I had not put them in. What if this operation was up in this area? I would be in trouble.

But Chittagong was now in sight. We had not flown close to it before and the town was a bit bigger than I expected. The airfield was on a spit of land a few miles to the south. I could now see the runway as Geoff followed quite closely behind Steve to land on it. It was a 'metallised' runway, constructed of interlocking steel plates, quite different to the grass field we had been operating from to date at Bhatpara. It was more of a proper airbase with a number of buildings and quite a few aircraft, mostly American B.25 Bombers and some P.38 Fighters parked about.

We were guided to a dispersal point and as soon as we clambered out of the aircraft a waiting truck whisked the four of us away to the briefing room. I entered it with some trepidation, but I need not have worried. In twenty minutes we were out again – surely the shortest briefing ever. They simply told us that there had been a report of a concentration of about a hundred barges in the coastal area a few miles north of Taungup. We were to search the area and try to locate and attack them. Of course we plied them with questions like, "what sort of barges?" and "are there any tugs or larger vessels?" but they just didn't know.

We got back into our aircraft and took off around 1445 hours. I was feeling a bit relieved because, by comparison with some of the places I feared we might have been sent, this trip seemed as though it would be a bit of a doddle.

But it wasn't.

The first part was easy. We flew down the Arakan coast, keeping low over the sea, to Oyster Island. We kept several miles to seaward of the island, so as to give the Japanese held port of Akyab on the mainland a wide berth. Then it was about 35 more minutes on to the Cheduba straits, a channel of water about seven miles wide between the large offshore islands of Ramree and Cheduba. Both these islands had garrisons of occupying Japanese forces and were known to have quite strong anti-aircraft defences. On reaching the south end of Cheduba we swung round eastwards and within a few minutes we were over the ill-defined coastline a few miles north of Taungup.

This area was a mass of mangrove swamps, criss-crossed by a few larger waterways but mostly a great number of small channels and creeks. Steve and Geoff had decided to keep in R/T contact as we both turned north over the specified area, flying on parallel tracks about five miles apart. However, we found that it was very difficult to see up and down some of the narrow waterways, particularly where there were overhanging mangrove trees. Geoff decided that we must climb up several hundred feet to look around. We did – and were immediately hit by small arms fire.

The sound made by a bullet piercing the stressed aluminium alloy of the fuselage was sharp, like someone filling a paper bag with air and bursting it. I was to hear this sound several times more in the next forty minutes because in order to search the area thoroughly we had to continue in the same manner, skimming across the treetops for a few minutes then pulling up to 500 feet or more, weaving violently to put any gunners of aim, whilst scanning the numerous creeks.

Steve also called to say that he too was getting a lot of flak. We knew that there would be enclaves of Japanese troops in this area but we were surprised at the amount of firing. Only two days previously we had been in this same area, patrolling a small coastal road that led from Taungup northwards and we had not been fired on once, even when we attacked and blew up a small bridge that carried the road over a little river at a village called Sabin.

After about forty minutes, during which time we had flown up and down the area four times, we concluded that there was no concentration of 'barges'. All that we had seen was a few odd sampans, which probably just contained Burmese fisherman, so we did not attack. This meant we still had our unused RPs slung under the wings but it was not considered advisable to return to base with them, as they might become a hazard in event of any mishap on landing, so a general instruction was to try and find an alternative military target for them.

At this point Steve said over the R/T, "I know where we can dump the RPs, Vardi. Follow me." He didn't mention Taungup by name but we guessed that's where he meant. We followed him a few miles southward, where we picked up the coast road that led to Taungup. Just outside the town, he fired his whole salvo of eight rockets into a group of buildings thought to be a storage dump and MT park. He knew this but, at the time, we didn't. Nevertheless, we followed up with a second attack.

As we retreated speedily out to sea I looked back and saw that the whole building complex was well and truly on fire. The amazing thing was that not a shot was fired at either of us. Notwithstanding the fact that we had been stooging around the same area a few miles north for about forty minutes and that, surely, they would have received some warning that two Beaufighters were nearby, we appeared to have taken them completely by surprise. It was around 1700 hours when we made the attack – perhaps it was Japanese 'tea time'!

We made the 300-odd mile journey back without incident and landed at Bhatpara at 1855 hours, about 15 minutes before nightfall. We had a short meeting with the Intelligence Officer, who noted our negative report. Amongst ourselves, we concluded that either they had sent us to the wrong area or, more likely, the report had been false and that there never had been a large group of 'barges'.

Before I went to sleep that night, I told myself that I should be more ready to expect the unexpected. Still... at least tomorrow would be a rest day – *probably!*

7.   The Taungup Pass

The Taungup Pass provided a way through the southern Arrakan Hills, where a tortuous road linked the railway terminal at Prome, on the Irrawaddy River, with Taungup, on the low-lying marshy coastline. It was therefore a vital route for the Japanese, who used it to get men, vehicles and supplies through to the garrison at Taungup. From there, the defensive positions on the large offshore islands of Ramree and Cheduba could be supported. Also, men and equipment could be moved northwards to reinforce positions in the Kaladan valley and Akyab. For these reasons it was heavily defended by medium ack-ack and numerous machine gun posts along its route.

For much of the pass, the road itself did not run in the bottom of the valley but high up along the edges of even higher, steep hillsides. In many places it was obscured by trees and jungle, making it difficult to observe any vehicles moving on it or to spot any defensive gun positions hidden in the undergrowth. It was a dangerous place to stooge around, looking for targets – they could see *you* but often you could not see *them* until they opened fire. Enemy convoys travelled mostly at night and although their headlights would make them visible, these would be extinguished as soon as they were attacked. Low-level attacks by Beaufighters at night were not practical and would be very dangerous within the confines of the pass, so patrols were usually carried out at dawn on the coastal end of the pass, where the road descended to low-level and where vehicles might be caught before they reached the relative safety of dispersal points in or around the heavily-defended town of Taungup itself.

By mid-May Geoff and I had completed six operational flights and we were beginning to feel a bit more experienced. Nevertheless, I did have a few qualms when, on the afternoon of 16th May, we, together with another crew (F/S Gamlin and

W/O Mearns) were briefed to do a patrol along the Taungup Pass from the coastal end. Furthermore, we were to arrive at the pass at first light, which would mean a pre-dawn take-off – our first night take-off from this grass field at Bhatpara.

Accordingly, we went to our aircraft early next morning in the unfamiliar darkness, dimly and eerily lit by a single row of flickering gooseneck flares, which marked the line of take-off. Engines started, both aircraft taxied to one end of the field. F/S Gamlin, who was a bit more experienced than Geoff, was to be leader. He took off at 0330 hours followed by Geoff about a minute later. We had decided that we would try to keep together and initially F/S Gamlin kept his navigation lights on until Geoff had caught up with him. From then on Geoff was able to keep him in sight by the glow from his exhausts.

We flew at about 2,500 feet, following the coastline all the way down to the Naf peninsula. This was familiar terrain but it was the first time we had flown over it in the dark – and it really was dark. The sky above was overcast, so no stars were visible. On the ground there were a few twinkling lights from villages but the only identifiable places were at Feni, Chittagong and Cox's Bazaar. At the Naf peninsula we dropped down to about 300 feet above sea level and altered course slightly, aiming for the Cheduba Straight, between the offshore islands of Ramree and Cheduba. We reached the southern end of the Straight at about 0500 hours and swung round due east to cross the low-lying marshy coast a few miles south of the heavily-defended town of Taungup itself.

Although it was now daylight, visibility was poor, due to the still overcast sky and some rain showers. Nevertheless, we soon sighted the road and began to follow it as it ascended south-eastward into the hills. After a few more minutes, we found ourselves flying in a valley with steep wooded hills rising on both sides and a ceiling of low cloud swirling overhead. The road, which was on our right hand side and cut into the steep hill face about two thirds of the way up, was still visible occasionally through gaps in the trees but we saw no vehicles on it. However, it became obvious that we were not going to get much further as the road ahead was disappearing into a misty wall of cloud. F/S Gamlin, who was leading, called Geoff and warned him that he was turning to port and heading back whilst there was still room. We saw him go by and Geoff too had just started to turn when we saw an amazing sight.

Literally out of the clouds, several vehicles emerged, driving slowly with headlights on. It was the head of a Japanese military convoy! They had no doubt been driving overnight, intending by now to have reached the comparative safety of the Taungup dispersal areas, but must have been delayed by the poor visibility.

Geoff quickly reversed his turn and now, banking sharply to the right, positioned the aircraft to make an attack. Looking along the top of the fuselage, I glimpsed the leading vehicle, similar to a jeep, with a driver and what looked like two officers in the back. Behind this was a slightly larger vehicle, open-backed and with an anti-aircraft gun mounted on a supporting frame. Several soldiers were sitting down in it, obviously unaware of our presence at that moment. Following were three large military transport vehicles. Geoff opened fire on these and then, as he turned seawards, raked the whole column right up to the leading jeep with one sustained burst of cannon fire. As we retreated, I looked backward and saw that one of the transports had virtually exploded in a ball of fire and that several other fires had started.

Then there occurred a flurry of R/T calls between Geoff and F/S Gamlin. Geoff called him to come back, keeping to the north side of the valley, and make a follow-up attack. We would keep to the south side until we saw them pass, which they did a few minutes later. We turned around and followed them, ready to make the next attack, but as we got back to the scene there was hardly a vehicle left that was not already blazing. F/S Gamlin had set fire to several more of them at the rear, where the cloud above seemed to have temporarily lifted, no doubt due to the heat of the burning fires, leaving them like sitting ducks with nowhere to go. As we retreated again along the south hillside, I looked back on a scene of utter devastation. Vehicles and even some trees were burning everywhere. The ceiling of low cloud above us was blood red with reflections of the flames.

However, my enduring memory today is that of seeing one of the leading jeep-type vehicles that we had attacked as it first appeared out of the cloud. It had run off the road and tumbled about thirty feet down the steep hillside, where it had come to rest, still blazing, on its side, wedged against a very stout tree. Several soldiers were scattered around it, either dead or injured. A bit lower down, another appeared to be clinging desperately to a shrub to prevent sliding several hundred feet further down the steep hill face.

This was the ugly face of war.

After returning for one more brief look, the cloud seemed to be descending again and it was evident that no more vehicles would emerge, as the road ahead of them was blocked. It was a very dangerous place to be because of the high risk of collision between our two aircraft in such a confined area. I had to try to estimate the number of vehicles destroyed whilst at the same time obeying Geoff's instruction to keep the other Beaufighter in sight at all times. It was very difficult!

Geoff and F/S Gamlin soon decided to head back towards the sea and return the way we had come. The flight back was uneventful. At debriefing there was some feeling of success but also of disappointment. If our sortie had been timed about half an hour later we would have caught them lower down on the more exposed coastal road into Taungup and could then have dealt the enemy a much more severe blow.

8.   Convoy Escort

Our operational flying from Feni had settled down to a familiar pattern of briefing in the late afternoon for a sortie the next day. This normally gave me time in the evening to study the route to the target area, particularly the section where we would be low flying. I was, by now, quite used to low-level map reading and it did not worry me whether we would be climbing over the Chin hills and down on to the central plain or, as we sometimes did, flying over the sea a few miles off the coast and then turning inland to reach the target area.

However, on 7th June we were briefed for a sortie that was to be quite different. We were to fly out to sea to find and escort a small convoy of five ships, which were sailing up the Bay of Bengal towards the mouths of the Ganges. Its last reported position, the previous evening, was 21° 20' N and 91° 35' E and it was to be escorted by three Beaufighters in turn, each staying with it for two hours until it reached the beginning of the Sandwip Channel, where American P38 fighters from Chittagong would take over. Geoff and I would do the first two hours, taking off at 0530 hours.

We were going to have to locate this convoy, which might mean doing a bit of serious navigation for a change, so that evening, instead of planning a low-level track across Burma, I spent a worrying couple of hours swotting up the Navigation Manual on interception of convoys.

We had not been given any information about the course and speed of the ships, other than that they were heading for Sandwip, which would mean them sailing virtually due north. From Feni to the reported position was almost due south, which should make it easy, as we would be meeting head-on, but we were now well into the Monsoon period and if it was raining, with poor visibility, we might easily miss them and I would have to be prepared to do a square search.

Next morning Geoff and I took off at 0534 in aircraft NE.366 T and set course for my calculated position out to sea. It was just getting light and I was pleased to find that, although the sky was overcast, it was not raining for a change and the visibility was fair. At least ten minutes before ETA Geoff spotted a smudge of smoke on the horizon and altered course towards it. A few minutes later we were over them. They were somewhat further inshore than we had expected but I was relieved that we had found them so easily.

The leading cargo vessel was fairly large and looked in good condition but the other four, strung out behind it, were a motley collection, looking a bit the worse for wear. Spread out round the convoy were five escort vessels of the Indian Navy. Only one could be described as a corvette, whilst the others were small patrol launches, probably only lightly armed. We were under instructions to maintain R/T and W/T silence but as we flew over the leading ship I asked Geoff if I should try to contact them by signal lamp and he agreed.

I had with me an Aldis lamp which, although a standard piece of RAF equipment, we did not normally carry because they were in short supply on the squadron. The Aldis lamp was like a large, battery-operated torch, with about a five-inch reflector. It was held by a handle at the back with a trigger which, when pulled, mechanically aligned the reflector to give a full beam. When the trigger was released the spring-loaded reflector returned to its normal misaligned position and the recipient would only see a faint light. Thus the trigger enabled short or long flashes of light, corresponding to letters in Morse Code, to be sent. Along the top of the lamp there was a sight, similar to a gunsight, to look through, so it could be kept trained on the recipient.

I had practised sending messages by Aldis lamp back in 1942 on Initial Training Wing at the Devon seaside resort of Babbacombe. We would pair up with someone standing at the opposite end of the grass esplanade in front of the row of cliff-top hotels and send messages (sometimes rude!) to each other until we were competent to do this at speeds of up to 18 words per minute or more. However, neither in subsequent operational training on Beaufighters, nor since commencing operations on 211 Squadron, had I ever had occasion to use an Aldis lamp.

As we flew past the leading vessel I trained the lamp at the bridge and flashed the words *"Good morning. All OK?"* I was somehow quite surprised when immediately the signal flashed back *"Yes thanks".* The signaller on the bridge was on the ball. Of course, he didn't know that this was a new experience for me, using an Aldis lamp for real for the first time.

We then flew on and made a couple of circuits round the perimeter of the entire convoy. I scanned the sea in all directions and it was empty. At briefing I had asked why the convoy needed protection and against what possible threat, but the only answer we got was that the Indian Navy had asked for it. There were no Japanese naval forces known to be this far up in the Bay of Bengal, nor at the nearest enemy-held port of Akyab on the Arrakan coast, except, possibly, a couple of lightly-armed motor launches.

After about an hour, and god knows how many circuits, we both admitted that it was becoming rather boring. At this point, I recall Geoff commenting that maybe it was just as well that we had not been posted to do our operations on a Coastal Command squadron in the UK after all. He was referring to the fact that during training, both on Hampdens in Canada and Beaufighters at Crosby-on-Eden, our courses had been orientated towards Coastal Command work. We had expected to be posted to a Coastal Command squadron in the UK, where we may well have experienced quite a few uneventful protection patrols such as this.

Then, after we had been droning around for about one and a half hours, still scanning the sea in all directions, I happened to be looking south towards Akyab when I spotted a small, yellow object in the water, about fifteen miles away. I drew Geoff's attention to it and he said he thought it might be a dinghy and we ought to go and have a look. As he turned the aircraft towards it and away from the convoy I thought they would be wondering what we were doing, so I flashed a message *"something in sea",* which they acknowledged. I thought afterwards that this might have worried them a bit, as they may have thought it was a mine!

As we flew towards it, Geoff said it was definitely yellow but didn't look like a dinghy. Indeed, we were almost over it before we were able to identify it. It was a dead cow! It was floating upside down with its legs rigid in the air. Its bloated belly was distinctly yellow and it had probably been in the water for some time. We turned back towards the convoy, discussing theories as to how this surreal object came to be so far out to sea.

As we flew back over the convoy, the leading vessel flashed the message *"What was it?"*

I flashed back the answer, *"A dead cow!"*

There was no immediate response. In fact, there followed what seemed to be a pregnant pause of about a minute. Possibly what I had said was so unexpected that the signaller doubted if he had read it correctly, or maybe my use of the exclamation mark flummoxed him. (In Morse Code an exclamation mark is the letters GW run together which, as light flashes, would be long-long-short-short-long-long, but in operational messages exclamation marks were rarely used.) Maybe he had to look it up or even thought I was joking. Eventually he signalled for me to repeat the message which I did, and received an acknowledgment.

We resumed our circuits round the convoy until I noted that we had been with it for two hours, when I began looking expectantly northwards, in the direction of Feni, for the Beaufighter which was to relieve us – but there was no sign of it. Geoff said that we should stay until it arrived, but it never came. After another hour he decided that we should return to base and I had one more brief exchange of messages with that unknown signaller on the Commodore's ship, telling him that we must leave now. He acknowledged it with thanks.

We returned to Feni, landing at 0939 hours, and it was then that we found out that the crew who should have relieved us had reported sick (at that time, quite a few aircrew were experiencing bouts of sickness and diarrhoea). Geoff and I had been lucky in not being affected by this bug but it did mean we were having to fly more frequently. We had to fly again on the 10th and 11th – by which time we had done three operations in four days. Normally, with the full complement of crews available on 'B' Flight, we would have had a gap of two to three days between each operational flight.)

Still, this convoy escort duty had been something completely different for us, and I had gained the experience of using an Aldis lamp to communicate with a ship at sea for the first time – even if it had only been to report the sighting of a dead cow!

The Author on leave with 'Hoppy' and 'China', December 1944.

9. Crash at Chittagong

When we joined 211 Squadron, in mid-April 1944, they were operating from a small grass landing strip near Bhatpara, a village about seven miles from Comilla. It was known that the Squadron would have to move when the Monsoon rains started because the ground would become too soft. I had wondered about the Monsoons but found that nobody seemed to know exactly when and how the rains would start, and to what extent they would interfere with operational flying. This was because the Squadron, which had originally flown Blenheims, had only been re-formed towards the end of 1943, after having been wiped out in Java. The present Squadron had been equipped with Beaufighter Mk.Xs, trained in firing Rocket Projectiles at Silchar, and moved to Bhatpara only recently.

To begin with, the weather was fine and did not present any problems, even flying over the Chin Hills, which we had to do on almost every trip to get to targets in the central plains of Burma. Indeed, at certain times the air was so crystal clear over these mountains that we could see for nearly 80 miles from a height of about 9,000 feet. However, towards the end of the month the weather at Bhatpara changed. Although the days usually started with clear skies there would be a build-up of cumulus clouds, quite heavy by mid-afternoon and threatening rain, but not a drop fell.

When the order for the Squadron to move eventually came, early in May, it came with very short notice. So short, in fact, that one morning, just as Geoff and I were about to take-off on a sortie, for which we had been briefed the previous evening, our 'B' Flight OC came dashing up in a jeep with a last-minute instruction. We were not to return to Bhatpara but were to land at Feni, an airfield about 25 miles to the south. He said all the aircraft were to be flown there that very morning, while we were away, and we each had to nominate someone whom we would make responsible for packing and safely transporting our belongings.

During the next few weeks, operating from Feni, the weather got progressively worse, but it was an 'all-weather' airfield, which had a runway constructed with interlocking perforated steel plates that enabled quite large aircraft to use it, even when the ground underneath was waterlogged. Also, it had a proper Control Tower and R/T communication with a range of about 25 miles (in contrast with Bhatpara, where the only 'Flying Control' was a Duty Pilot in a tent with an Aldis signal lamp!). Other units were also operating from Feni, including some American forces engaged on transporting supplies 'over the hump' to China, so the place was much busier than we had been used to.

At this time, our sorties into enemy territory were mostly to the Monywa and Pakkoku regions of Burma, which lay some 300 miles to the south east. We would take-off, often in rain, with poor visibility, and climb steadily to about 9,000 feet. Generally, we would break through cloud into clear air at around 5,000 feet, but ahead of us would be a formidable line of cloudbanks over the Chin Hills. Some of these clouds towered up way above the maximum ceiling of a Beaufighter, which was about 10,000 feet under such atmospheric conditions. We had to thread our way through these because we had been well warned of the dangers of flying in cumulo-nimbus clouds over the mountains.

Once on the other side, the cloud-tops over the plains would be lower and we would generally be able to find gaps through which we could descend and proceed to our target areas by low-level map reading. On the return journey, we would, of course, have to face the same hazards of flying over the mountains again. However, in spite of the worsening monsoon weather, of the eleven trips we did during May only once did we return without having completed our mission.

In June, conditions got worse and there were reports of extensive flooding along the Arakan coast south of Feni, in the regions of Chittagong and Cox Bazaar. I had a fear that one day the weather conditions around our base would deteriorate while we were away and that we would be unable to find it and land safely.

Before long, on the 15th of June to be exact, my worst fear was realised! We had taken off at 0755 hours, our task being to patrol a section of the Irrawaddy from Allenmyo to Chauk. We had crossed the Chin Hills as usual but as we descended and made our way to the river we encountered quite a lot of low cloud and rain. As we began our patrol, visibility worsened but we pressed on. Our perseverance paid off, as we found and attacked up to ten *kisties* that were making their way upstream, perhaps heading for the Chindwin and on to Kalewa. No doubt they thought that in such poor weather they would be safe from attack.

We flew on for a bit but became concerned about the weather and decided to cut short our patrol and head back to base. But we had left it a bit too late...

Half way back over the mountains it became clear that the weather had worsened rapidly since we had left. Normally, we were completely cut off from any communication with base whilst low flying over Burma because we were out of R/T range, even with Cox's Bazaar, and I could neither send or receive any signals on my W/T set from Feni or Agatala because of the intervening hills. However, now that we were high enough, I became aware of a babble of Morse messages in my earphones and sensed that something was amiss. American cargo aircraft were being diverted to land at Dacca instead of Agatala or Feni. Almost at the same time, Geoff heard a faint R/T message passing from one aircraft to another, indicating that the airfields at Feni, Chittagong and Cox's Bazaar were all unfit for landing, due to low cloud and poor visibility.

I estimated that we were somewhere about Kaladan, where there was a river running north and south in a deep gorge, which would usually enable me to pinpoint our position, but today it was completely obscured. We were now at about 5,000 feet, just above a sea of cumulus cloud stretching unbroken as far as we could see, and it did not look as though there would be much hope of finding any gaps. Also, the sky above was becoming more overcast, with a layer of altostratus cloud, which looked as though it was becoming progressively lower ahead of us. In other words, we were in trouble!

Geoff said he wanted to try and descend through the cloud as soon as possible, but I was not sure enough of our position. There were still quite a number of high spots in the foothills below, between us and Feni. I suggested that we altered course, flying due west for about 10 minutes, by which time we should have cleared all the foothills to the west of us. We could then safely descend to 1,500 feet over the flat coastal area around Chittagong. If this did not get us below the cloud-base then another 10 minutes flying should ensure that we were heading out to sea before reducing height further. Once we made visual contact with the sea, we could turn back to the coast and follow it northwards towards Feni. We decided to try this.

At 1,500 feet we were still in cloud and had to continue, heading out to sea. The last five minutes was nerve-wracking as we edged down lower and lower, peering through the gloom until, at about 700 feet, we saw the sea, whereupon we did a steep about-turn, heading back towards the coast. I could see whitecaps and wind lanes on the surface, indicating a very strong wind from the south, which was causing the rain to beat almost horizontally against our starboard side. It was bumpy and almost as dark as nightfall, but the whitecaps helped us to maintain visual contact with the sea.

After the few minutes or so that I had estimated it would take us to reach the shore, I was taken aback to notice that we were flying over flooded paddy fields. This part of the Arakan coast was flat and rather featureless at the best of times but I now realised that the flooding was so bad that there was no visible demarcation between the sea and the water-covered low-lying land. Also, I had not seen the railway that ran northwards, parallel to the shore, two or three miles inland. Was it under water? I wondered. Worse still, were we so far away from where I thought we were as to be *south* of Chittagong, where there was no railway? I was just beginning to panic when Geoff said he could see some lights and, as he turned towards them, we were relieved to realise that it was the town of Chittagong. This enabled us to orientate ourselves and head for the airfield, which we knew to be on a flat spit of land a few miles south of the town.

Like Feni, Chittagong had only one runway, which lay roughly east/west and we knew that the gale-force crosswind from the south would make landing very tricky. Nevertheless, it made sense to try to put down here rather than attempt to get back to base in such atrocious weather. After a few minutes, Geoff caught sight of the runway through the blinding rain and low cloud, in fact it lay straight ahead of us as we were approaching from the seaward end. He called on the R/T and requested permission to make an immediate emergency landing. There was some delay, indeed by the time the air controller replied he had already got the undercarriage and flaps down. The air controller warned us that the airfield had already been closed as unfit for use, that there was a 45-knot crosswind gusting to 60 knots and that there was a lot of water on the first third of the runway. Nevertheless, he gave us permission to attempt a landing, but added an ominous phrase I had never before heard from an air controller, "Use extreme caution."

We approached in a crabwise fashion, banking and turning into the fiercely gusting wind, and it took all Geoff's skill to keep in line with the runway. Visibility was poor and, of course, there were no lights. To make matters worse, the water was obscuring the edges of the runway, so he had no nearby visual reference points to guide him in the difficult manoeuvre of straightening up just before touchdown. Unfortunately, just at the critical moment, there were two violent gusts in rapid succession, which may have caused him to over correct and also, I believe, lifted the starboard wing. In the event, we hit the runway rather heavily, on the skew, and the port undercarriage leg gave way.

Next, quite unexpectedly, because we had not realised that it could have been so deep, a great sheet of water shot right over the nose of the plane, reaching even the Perspex cover of my cupola. For the next second or two, Geoff could see nothing until the water drained from his cockpit windscreen, during which time I could feel, from centrifugal force, that we were swerving round to the left. Indeed, at this point he realised that he no longer had any directional control and all he could do was to cut the engines as we careered, still partly airborne by the wind, which was now behind us, with a series of heavy bumps and splashes across the edge of the airfield, finally coming to rest on the adjacent flooded paddy fields.

We were both a bit shaken but unhurt and jumped out quickly, finding ourselves knee-deep in muddy water. We had scarcely spoken when we heard the drone of aero engines borne on the wind, which made us turn and look back at the runway, where we were dumfounded to see that an American B.25 Mitchell aircraft had landed from the opposite end. The B.25 was a heavier aircraft, with a tricycle undercarriage, and had obviously made a better touchdown than we had, but at that moment it was still moving quite fast as it swished into the flooded section of the runway from which we had just come. There was no doubt in my mind that, had we not almost literally been blown off the runway but continued along it, we would have crashed head-on and almost certainly been killed.

Geoff became angry that the Air Controller had given us permission to land without even warning us that there was another aircraft in the area, let alone one that was attempting to land from the *opposite* direction, and he would certainly 'give him an earful' at the earliest opportunity. Meanwhile, we were rapidly getting soaked to the skin and could do nothing but try and shelter against the side of the fuselage, waiting for someone to come. It was nearly ten minutes before anyone did, and then it was only two airmen in a jeep, who stopped about 200 yards away on the perimeter track and walked gingerly through the water, trying to locate the submerged paths. I could not help contrasting this situation with that of our crash at Crosby-on-Eden the previous February, when a crash tender and ambulance reached us within a minute. However, no doubt here the crews of the emergency vehicles had been stood down, as there was not supposed to be any flying taking place.

They helped us get our parachutes, etc, out of the aircraft and as we made our way to the jeep I glanced back at

Beaufighter NE.317, which looked in a sorry state. The propellers were bent and the port undercarriage support had given way completely so that the plane was tilted over with the wingtip submerged in muddy water. The wing itself was damaged, as it had hit the ground several times, and I doubt that this aircraft ever flew again.

We were taken first to the control tower, where Geoff went to confront the Air Controller, but the latter promptly took the wind out of his sails by immediately apologising and stating that the B.25 had appeared without any warning or attempt to make R/T contact, and that he would certainly be reporting the incident. The aircraft itself was still at the far end of the runway, awaiting some help to guide it to where it could park without sinking into the mud, therefore we did not get to meet the crew. This was probably just as well, as I don't think it would have done much to improve Anglo-American relations, which were already rather poor at the time.

Next, we were taken to the administration building, where we found that it was not possible to telephone through to Feni, as a number of lines were down. Instead, we arranged for a wireless signal to be sent to the squadron to let them know that we were safe. Then we started to discuss what we should do. Although Feni was only about 55 miles away, they said that transport could not be provided to take us back by road, and besides, it had been reported that the road was impassable at some points. It looked as though we would have to stay overnight and hope that the weather next day would improve enough for our squadron to send a Beaufighter to fetch us. We had landed (or 'pranged' – as such a mishap was known in RAF jargon) at 1140 hours, after having been airborne for 3 hours 45 minutes. We were still in our flying gear, wet through, tired and hungry. My spirits fell at the dismal prospect of having to stay overnight in makeshift accommodation, with borrowed clothes (if we were lucky) and not even any money to buy a drink in the Mess.

Then, suddenly, there was a ray of hope. Someone had telephoned the railway station at Chittagong and found that, surprisingly, in view of the widespread flooding, 'the train' was still running. This, we were told, was a local train that ran each day from Chittagong to Comilla, passing through Feni. It was now 1230 hours and the train was due to leave in about 40 minutes from the station, which was some 8 miles away. If we were to catch it, things would have to happen fast, and they did. A 15cwt truck was requisitioned, a corporal driver was found and hastily-scribbled railway warrants were thrust into our hands as we were bundled into it and driven off at high speed towards Chittagong.

By the time we got to the outskirts of the town, the gale had moderated somewhat and the rain had reduced to a steady drizzle. Nevertheless, I was surprised at the number of people in the streets. But then, I suppose living in a climate like this one can't wait until it stops raining before going out and about one's daily business. Our driver obviously knew the quickest way to the station through the backstreets but, in spite his frequent use of the horn, our progress was considerably slowed as he edged his way past chickens, children, coolies and women with seemingly impossible loads on their heads, people on bicycles, handcarts, rickshaws and so on, not to mention the occasional sacred cow standing stubbornly in the centre of the road.

I knew it was going to be touch-and-go as to whether we would catch the train but there was nothing I could do but sit in the back of the truck and gaze in wonder at the amazing human spectacle unfolding before me. I say 'amazing' because, although I had been in India for two months, this was the first time I had ever seen the backstreets of a sizeable town. As we passed by the miscellany of dwellings, some little more than shanties with corrugated iron roofs, interspersed with other, rather grander-looking houses, I became very aware that all around life was going on as it had done for generations. Perhaps, somewhere, a baby was being born or an old person was dying – but there were no visible signs of the war in which we were involved.

I was shaken out of my reverie as the truck pulled up with a jolt at the railway station, just at the time the train was due to leave. There was no time for the nicety of exchanging our warrants for tickets, so we rushed past a protesting ticket inspector onto the platform. Our corporal ran up and spoke to the guard, who directed him to a compartment that had, apparently, been reserved for military personnel. We hurried up to it and found that it was occupied by four army Subalterns, ensconced one in each corner, smartly dressed in their best khaki uniforms, complete with highly-polished Sam Brownes. As the corporal opened the door for us, one of the Subalterns protested. "You can't come in here. This compartment is reserved for officers!" Nevertheless, we staggered in, with our parachutes and harnesses, I with my canvas navigator's bag, into which I had also stuffed our flying helmets and some other items salvaged from the plane. Geoff told them that we were RAF officers, as I shouted our thanks to the corporal and shut the door as the train started.

To say that they were annoyed by our intrusion would be an understatement, but their looks of annoyance changed more to alarm as they took a good look at us. We were dressed, as we normally were for operational flights over Burma, in what were called Beedon suits. These were one piece overalls like boiler suits, in self-coloured olive green, but not camouflaged because they were not intended to be combat suits but rather jungle survival suits. As such, they bulged with numerous pockets, into which were stowed emergency food packs, medicines, first aid kit, matches, marching compass, spare socks, fishing line with hooks, razor and so on. Around our waists we wore grey webbing belts with a revolver in a holster attached to the left side and on the right an ammunition pouch and a rather lethal-looking dagger. Also, in a long calf pocket in the right leg of our suits we carried a special type of folding kukri, rather like a giant penknife, where the handle protected the razor-sharp, curved blade.

Add to this that we displayed no badges of rank or aircrew insignia and wore heavy black marching boots on our feet, which were covered in mud as though we had just marched out of the jungle, it was no wonder that they viewed us with suspicion. Were we Deserters? Bandits? Mercenaries? Or were some military manoeuvres taking place in the area that they did not know about? By the looks on their faces, I imagined such thoughts must have been running through their heads. It took quite a while to convince them that we really were who we said we were, after which they became friendlier.

It turned out that they were from units being held in reserve south of Cox's Bazaar, and were on their way to a Conference in Comilla, where they were also spending a few days leave, hence the best uniforms. When they realised that, only a few hours before, we had been flying over Japanese-held territory, far beyond the positions held by them, they became very interested and plied us with questions. Some of these we answered, but when one of them wanted me to show him on my map where we had been and what we had seen that particular morning I declined, saying that we had not yet reported to our Intelligence Officer. This cooled relations a little, after which the conversation turned to the appalling weather and the dreariness of the journey.

It was still raining and there was extensive flooding on both sides of the track. The train trundled on painfully slowly. There were thirteen stations, mostly tiny halts, between Chittagong and Feni and it stopped for long periods at each one, as well as numerous stops in between. At one station we got out to stretch our legs and found that they had actually uncoupled the engine and sent it on ahead to check that the line was passable to the next station. At first this seemed to us to be ridiculous, but the Guard explained that there had been reports that water was lapping over the track ahead, and it was better to risk the engine getting marooned between stations rather than a trainload of passengers. It was over an hour before the engine came back and the train got under way again.

When we had first boarded the train I had expected that we would be back at base within, at most, three hours and in time for our evening meal in the Mess. How wrong I was! The rest of the journey dragged on interminably and my hunger and sheer boredom were relieved only by occasionally dozing off to sleep. I do not recall clearly our actual arrival at Feni, except that it was dark and about 2200 hours. The airfield was only about five miles from the station but I remember sitting around for a long time whilst Geoff, with the help of the local military RTO, did some telephoning. For some reason it was not possible to get through to the Squadron directly and it took a long time before he could contact anyone who could authorise sending transport to collect us. Eventually a truck came and took us back to our base camp.

It was a few minutes to midnight when I was dropped off at the little path that led to my bamboo Basha, the same point where I had been picked up by a jeep to be taken to the dispersal point to board the Beaufighter some seventeen hours ago. It had been a very long day and I was exhausted and very hungry. I shared this Basha with my friends China Whale and Tubby Thompson and two others but the place was in darkness as they were all asleep. Trying not to make too much noise, I found the matches and lit the hurricane lamp and I felt a slight sense of annoyance when I saw that the mosquito net on my charpoy had not been put down. This should have been done by our Bearer, a local Bengali lad paid by us to generally look after the place and run errands, and the only reason he would not have put it down was if he had been told not to bother – perhaps 'because Sahib is not coming back'.

Then it dawned on me that maybe they did not know that we had made it back over mountains to Chittagong and it was soon confirmed that this was indeed the case when a bleary-eyed, white-faced and confused-looking China peeped out from under his mosquito net.

"Is that you Denny?" he said, incredulously. "We thought you were a goner!" I assured him that he was not dreaming, nor was I a ghost. The noise woke the others, who crawled out of bed to shake my hand and congratulate me as though I really had come back from the dead. Somebody produced a bottle of gin and we all had a celebratory drink, albeit out of enamelled mugs and diluted only with water, notwithstanding the fact that they had spent the evening in the Mess drinking and commiserating over what they thought was the loss of yet another aircrew. I learned later that the signal from Chittagong had eventually filtered through from

Wing headquarters to our Commanding Officer late in the evening but that no news of it had reached the NCOs' Mess.

Finally, China helped me brush the moths and other creepy crawlies, attracted by the light, from the top sheet and tuck in the mosquito net, and we all slumped back into our beds. Just before I sank into oblivion, I reflected that I was really beginning to understand how hazardous flying in the Monsoon period could be, and silently cursed Admiral Lord Mountbatten, the recently-appointed Allied Commander for South East Asia, who (from the relative safety and comfort of Government House in Calcutta!) had decreed: "There will be no drawing of stumps for this Monsoon".

Sequel

In the early 1960s I was working for Potterton International as Manager of their Appliance Development Laboratory at Wandsworth. This involved organising the test facilities, equipment and staff required to carry out trials on prototypes of new ranges of sectional cast iron central heating boilers, both gas and oil fired. At this time I had a staff of about seventeen development engineers, with different levels of qualification, but to cope with an expanding programme of work I needed another junior. Accordingly, I had arranged for an advertisement to be placed in a local paper, which had resulted in quite a large number of applications. These had been whittled down to a shortlist of five, who were asked to come for interviews.

Thus it came about that on a certain day the first of these, a young Indian lad named Mukerjee, was ushered into my office. He was a bit nervous and I chatted to him for a few minutes on general matters to put him at ease. I found out that he had come to England with his parents shortly after the war and all his schooling had been here. He spoke English very well and his handwriting was neat, as I saw from his application form, which I then started to read. He had 'O' levels in English, Maths and Physics, which is what we needed and, as a school leaver, he seemed to be just what I was looking for.

As I ran my eye over his personal details, the writing seemed to jump up at me and I felt a strange thrill of excitement as I noted that his place of birth was Chittagong, the year 1944, the month June, and the day? Yes, incredible though it seemed, at the same time as I had made my first dramatic acquaintance with Chittagong, he was being born!

I did, of course, have to interview four others and to make a choice, but in the end I gave the job to young Mukerjee. I admit that this strange karmic coincidence may have influenced me in his favour, but he proved to be a useful and diligent worker.

However, seeing him almost every day kept reminding me of things I wanted to forget – things that had happened at another time, in another place and in what now seemed like another world.

10. My Narrowest Escape

Although No. 211 Squadron was part of the Third Tactical Air Force, our role was not that of close tactical support but rather to penetrate deep into enemy-held territory and carry out offensive patrols along selected stretches of road, railway and river to deter the enemy from using them during daylight hours. Apart from the danger of being shot down by enemy fighters or anti-aircraft fire, there were additional hazards, due to the very nature of the terrain. The range of mountains known as the Chin Hills formed a natural barrier between the forward landing strips in the Arakan from which we operated and the central areas of Burma where our targets lay. On almost every trip, we had to climb over them, often in atrocious Monsoon weather.

Once over the mountains there were other dangers, such as the hazards of low flying for long periods, both to and from the target area. We flew at low-level to escape detection as far as possible and to avoid fire from larger ack-ack guns. We could still be, and often were, hit by light machine gun and even rifle fire. This meant that every time we flew over or near small villages or groups of buildings that might be occupied by Japanese soldiers Geoff would start 'weaving' – a rather violent combination of banking, turning and side-slipping – which made it more difficult for a gunner to apply the right deflection when aiming a weapon. Of course, all this was very tiring for Geoff and one slight misjudgement on his part could have resulted in disaster for us both, such as hitting a tree or flying into the ground. By the time we got back across the Chindwin river and started the long climb back over the mountains Geoff might have done as much as four hours of low flying.

Then there was the fear of the 'what if' scenarios. What if I were to be badly injured? There was no way that Geoff could render any first aid and it might be two or three hours flying back to base. Worse still, what if Geoff was injured or killed? Although I could crawl up the fuselage to the front and stand behind the pilot's seat, it was impossible to change places and in any case I could not fly a Beaufighter. What if I bailed out, or by some miracle survived a crash, and found myself alone, several hundred miles inside enemy-held territory? Although we wore survival suits and marching boots and carried a revolver and dagger, I doubt whether I, a town-bred Westerner, would have lasted more than a few days in such an alien and hostile environment as the jungle that covered much of northern Burma. What if I met some Burmese villagers? Even if they offered food and shelter, how could I be sure that they had not sent someone to fetch the nearest Japanese soldiers?

Then there was the vexed question of the money belt. On operational trips we wore a canvas money belt, into which were sewn 400 rupee coins, intended to pay Burmese people for any help they could give. However, we aircrews regarded the wisdom of this with a degree of scepticism. It was alright if you were alert and still had a revolver, but sooner or later you must sleep. Would they be able to resist the temptation to cut your throat, share out the money, and dispose of your body? After all, 400 rupees was equivalent to about two year's wages for the average peasant. And what if you were captured by the Japanese? Heaven help you if you had already been robbed of your money belt, because they would assume that you had hidden it somewhere and torture you until you revealed where it was.

On the other hand, if you *did* have it they would simply take the money – and anything else they wanted. Then, especially if it was in an area where it would be too much trouble to transport you to a labour camp, they would most likely kill you anyway. Finally, what if I was 'lucky' enough to be sent to a prisoner of war camp? In other theatres of war, this would mean being treated in accordance with the Geneva Convention, but the Japanese were not signatories to the Convention and to their way of thinking prisoners of war were dishonoured men. We had heard stories of how they treated them as virtual slave labourers, forcing both officers and men alike to work on construction projects under atrocious conditions.

We were all aware of these potential dangers but seldom talked about them. In retrospect, I wonder how I ever voluntarily climbed into the navigator's cockpit of a Beaufighter and set off on a sortie far behind enemy lines. But I did, again and again and again. Forty-nine times, in fact. Geoff and I were lucky in that neither of us received any injuries, although our aircraft was hit on a number of occasions by machine gun bullets and shrapnel. We always made it back, but there was one time, forever imprinted in my memory, when I myself missed death by inches and split seconds. Geoff might well have made it home by himself but with only dismembered bits of a navigator in the back.

On the afternoon of 7th July 1944 we were briefed for a trip on the following day to the Bassein delta area, which was well down to the South. I feared this region, not only because it was a long way away, some 400 miles from base, but also because we would be uncomfortably close to several landing strips at Bassein and Rangoon, where it was believed that some Japanese fighters were kept. Furthermore, the Burmese people in this part of the country were amongst the most hostile towards the British. However, there was the advantage that the area could be reached by flying all the way down the coast, a few miles offshore. Over the sea we could fly straight and level at about 200 feet, which was less hazardous and less tiring for Geoff than flying over the hills and across the plains in this Monsoon season of 1944.

Next morning we took off from Feni before dawn. We were in our 'favourite' Beaufighter – NE.298 – which bore the squadron letter 'V', but on this occasion we were not armed with rockets. Indeed, the rocket rails themselves had been temporarily removed to reduce drag and thereby lower petrol consumption. This was normal practice for long-range trips such as this one, which was expected to be of nearly six hours duration.

Unexpectedly, the weather was fairly good and we flew down the coast to Foul Island without any problems. Foul Island was a remarkable little island, probably of volcanic origin. It looked neatly round, about two miles diameter, and rose sharply some 150 feet out of the open sea. It was visible for quite some distance on this morning and provided a useful landmark to get my bearings in order to cross the coastline at the point where I had planned. When we reached the mainland we had to climb to about 3,000 feet to fly over the 'tail end' of the Chin Hills before reaching the flat area of the delta, where we began low flying.

After a few minutes we reached the railway, where it crossed the Bassein river, at a place called Nyogin Ferry. It was 0700 hours when we began our patrol along this section of line towards Henzada. There were two or three small stations or halts on the way but we saw nothing except a few derelict wagons at one of them. We always had to look at these carefully, as the Japanese sometimes parked loaded wagons, which may have been in transit during the night, amongst them. They would cunningly camouflage them with old bits of splintered wood, etcetera, to look like wagons previously attacked and damaged. Locomotives, which to them were virtually irreplaceable, were usually hidden away in the daytime in bomb-proof bunkers at places where there were convenient woods beside the track. Access would be via a short siding from points on the track so expertly camouflaged with foliage and rubble that they were very difficult to spot, even when low flying.

However, what we were hoping to find, at this early hour in the morning, was a train on the move.

It took about five minutes to reach Henzada, where the line had a short spur to a railhead on the west bank of the Irrawaddy – the place our Intelligence Officer had been interested in – but all was quiet and it appeared deserted. In the briefing room at Feni there was a large 'flack' map on the wall, which had coloured dots marking places where enemy fire had been experienced and which was continually being updated from reports by aircrews from all operational squadrons. Navigators would mark these places on their own maps for areas where they would be going. I had both heavy and light ack-ack symbols on my map for Henzada, which was known to be occupied by Japanese forces. Although the railhead was slightly south of the town, we were at a spot where we had expected some enemy opposition. But there was none.

We turned and flew northwards up the Irrawaddy towards a similar railhead, on the opposite bank, about three miles away. There was nothing to be seen here either and, as briefed, we followed this branch line for 18 miles to where it joined the main Rangoon to Prome railway at a town called Letpadan. We had planned to follow this line northwards, almost to Prome, before breaking off and heading back over the mountains. Letpadan was a town a bit smaller than Henzada and there had been no information about ack-ack batteries on our 'flack' map. Nevertheless, it was big enough to almost certainly have some Japanese troops garrisoned there and had we flown across it we would probably have encountered machine gun fire. Instead, we skirted round it to the south and east, taking a good look before swinging back to join the railway again, just north of the town.

At this point, an oil pipeline, which ran beside the railway, was clearly visible. This prompted Geoff to ask me if I knew the current state of the pipeline, that is, whether it was carrying oil or not, according to our latest Intelligence. This pipeline ran all the way to Prome and then followed the Irrawaddy river round to the oilfields at Yenangyaung and Chauk. These oilfields were still producing some oil at this time and, as I understood it, the Allied policy was not to do any more structural damage to production plant, which presumably they hoped to recapture before long, but rather to constantly attack and breach or set fire to the pipeline. Of course, the Japanese were continually repairing it, but at least it made it very difficult for them to transport oil down to Rangoon in any quantity. However, the pipeline had not been mentioned at our briefing so I could only say to Geoff that I was not sure.

"Shall we give it burst anyway then?" said Geoff.

The terrain was flat scrubland, with a few wooded areas. There were no villages or dwellings in sight and this seemed to be a good place to make an attack where there would not be any opposition.

"Yes," I replied, little knowing that the very timing of my remark almost signed my own death warrant. Geoff banked to the right, climbing up three or four hundred feet, then turned left and made a shallow dive towards the pipeline. I had swivelled my seat so that I was facing forwards, as I usually did when we made such an attack. This was because while we were diving I could see along the top of the fuselage and make an independent observation as to where the cannon shells struck and what damage was done. He gave a short burst with the four 20mm cannons. These fired mixed armour-piercing, high explosive and incendiary rounds at a rate of about 10 a second, with devastating results. I saw smoke and debris fly up and flashes from the incendiaries, but as we flattened out, I lost sight of the target before I could see whether there was any leakage of oil or real fire.

As we flashed over the railway, Geoff started to climb and turn to the right, intending to double back so that we could take a good look and assess the damage. I remember scribbling 0717 hours, the time of the attack, on my pad … and then it happened. Over the intercom I heard Geoff mutter "Christ!" Simultaneously, there was a tremendous bang. The whole aircraft shuddered and seemed to move sideways, just as if we had collided with something. It banked violently to the left, diving towards the ground, while a strong smell of petrol fumes wafted down the fuselage.

This was it, one of the worst of the 'what if' scenarios was actually happening. I was convinced that Geoff had been killed, or seriously injured, and that I was sitting helplessly in a pilotless Beaufighter, diving into the ground. Damage must have caused a massive leakage of petrol, so however we hit the ground we would explode in a ball of fire. There would be no escape! Events in my life really did rush through my mind with incredible speed, together with all sorts of reasons why I was too young to die. Simultaneously, I had the weirdest sensation that the real me was sitting on my shoulder, relatively unperturbed and ready to 'bale out' of my body. At this moment, I noticed a cloud of red soil dust swirl up from the port wing tip, which must have been only a few inches from the ground. Then, as though to prolong the agony, the plane seemed to level up.

"Are you O.K. Denny?" said Geoff. Never in our many hours of flying together, before or since, had I been so relieved to hear his voice.

"Yes!" I shouted, "but climb! I can smell petrol and we may have to bale out."

But Geoff, who had the advantage of knowing what had happened, and that the plane was still under his control, kept his cool. "I'll climb in a minute," he said, "but we'd better get out of range first. Are you sure it's petrol you can smell?"

Even as he spoke, I realised that, in the heat of the moment, I had jumped to the conclusion that the vapour was petrol – but it was not.

"No," I replied. "It must be hydraulic fluid."

Geoff was relieved to hear this because, although it might mean that we would have trouble with the flaps or undercarriage later, we were not in immediate danger, and he could continue low flying. It was only when I then asked him what he meant by 'getting out of range" that he realised I did not know what had happened.

He then explained that as he pulled up out of the dive he saw, too late, that he was turning directly towards a heavy ack-ack battery. There were at least two big guns in sandbagged emplacements, which had been hidden from view by some trees. He had seen the flash from the barrel of one, which was fired at virtually point-blank range. The shell had hit us, fortunately without exploding, before he had time to take the violent evasive action that he subsequently did. This had happened at the very moment that I had turned my head inside the cockpit to jot down the time on my pad and so I had not seen the guns.

We continued streaking along at low-level in a westerly direction for several minutes to get well clear of the area. Neither of us could see any damage from our respective cockpits, but the aircraft had received such a heavy blow that we had an uncomfortable feeling that something might go wrong at any minute as a delayed result. We therefore decided to abandon our patrol, make for the coast, and fly back over the sea, the way we had come. We had to cross the Irrawaddy again, at a point where it was a rather exposed stretch of sandbanks and water channels, also another branch of the railway, but we did not encounter any machine gun fire. From then on it was flat, relatively unpopulated marshland stretching to the hills, which we could now see ahead, so we began to climb.

By the time we reached the coast at Bluff Cape and set course for Oyster Island we were at about 5,000 feet. Any threat from fighters was now receding and over the sea we could keep out of range of any gunfire. We therefore decided it would be safer to stay at this altitude because if anything went wrong and we had to bale out or ditch in the sea at least I would be able to make contact by W/T with one of the monitoring stations and give our position.

The sky above was overcast, but visibility was quite good. At this unfamiliar height I could see the coastline and the offshore islands of Ramree and Cheduba and had no difficulty in keeping track of where we were. This meant that I now had time to look around more carefully inside the aircraft for any signs of damage. I crawled forward a bit to the small header tank for the hydraulic system, which was fixed on the left hand side of the fuselage. By unscrewing the filler cap and using a pencil as a dipstick, I established that it was empty. The pipe leading from it was undamaged as far as I was able see down to the point where it disappeared into the floor. This was not the bottom of the fuselage but a false floor, which covered the breach end of the cannons and extended backwards to the point where my seat was mounted. Any damage must therefore have been below this, where I could not see.

Geoff was optimistic that, although we had lost all the fluid from the make-up tank, there might be enough in the pumps and system to get the undercarriage down. However, he did not want to try it until we got nearer to base because, if it did work, we would have to fly the remainder of the journey with it down. Time then began to drag as we droned on for about an hour, everything seeming to be normal, except for the suspense of wondering whether or not we were going to be able to get the undercarriage down.

Finally, after we had passed Oyster Island and altered course slightly to converge with what was now 'friendly' coastline, Geoff decided to experiment. First, he selected 'flaps down' but there was no movement whatsoever. Then he selected 'undercarriage down' and gave an exclamation of excitement as the indicators showed that both legs had unlocked and started to move down. But they stopped half way and no further manipulation of the selector lever had any effect. Geoff decided to try getting them down by increasing the gravitational pull on them and went into a shallow dive, building up speed and then pulled the nose up very sharply, hoping that a combination of gravity and centrifugal force would cause the reluctant undercart to snap into the 'down' position. This manoeuvre had been known to work, but on this occasion it didn't.

Undaunted, Geoff said he would try again. This time he dived more steeply, reaching an even higher speed and pulled the nose up as hard as he could. I was pressed heavily into my seat with a force that must have been at least three G, but the undercarriage didn't budge.

This was it. Suspense gave way to a feeling of apprehension as I realised there was no way we were going to make a normal landing. We resumed flying straight and level, now over land. When we were about twenty-five minutes from Feni, Geoff made contact by R/T, giving them our ETA, which was 0930 hours, and warning them that we were going to have to make a crash landing. They replied immediately, asking how much fuel we had and Geoff told them we would have enough to remain airborne for just over an hour after reaching them.

By the time we arrived overhead we had reduced height to about 3,000 feet and Geoff was in constant contact with the Controller as we began to circle. Feni was quite a busy airfield at that time, particularly with American transport aircraft taking off or landing every ten minutes or so. The reason for their concern over our fuel margin soon became clear when they told us that they did not want us to make our crash landing on the runway but on a broad grass strip on the left hand side of it. However, there were several aircraft parked on it, which were in the process of being towed away, so we would have to circle until it was clear.

Meanwhile, they asked us to descend and make a low-level pass in front of the Control Tower whilst someone looked at the underside of our Beaufighter through binoculars. This we did, but it only confirmed what we already thought, that the undercarriage doors were just open and the wheels protruding by about half their diameter. As we flew along the line of the runway I saw small groups of personnel standing with their faces upturned. On an operational airfield like this, word spreads quickly that an aircraft is in trouble and they had no doubt come to see what sort of a job Geoff made of the landing. Oh, how I wished I was one of them, with my feet firmly on the ground!

We climbed up a bit and continued circling for what seemed like an eternity. Actually, it was only about another twenty minutes before the last aircraft was towed away and the grass verge was clear of obstructions. The Controller suggested that Geoff make a dummy run over the grass strip to take a good look at it first. As we did this, I was a bit alarmed to notice that at intervals there were some small drainage ditches, about 18 inches wide, running across it from the runway. Our wheels were partly down and would probably be forced back up into the nacelles as we hit the ground, but what if our point of touchdown coincided with one of these ditches? Would the wheels dig in? I began to have visions of the aircraft turning over and me being trapped upside down inside as it burst into flames.

Of course, Geoff had seen the ditches also and as he made no comment about them I assumed he was not worried, particularly as he then told the Controller that he would make one final circuit and then make his crash landing.

As we were on the downwind leg, he suddenly said to me "Do you want to bale out Denny? If you do, it's OK with me."

This took me completely by surprise, as I had not even considered the possibility. Was he worried about these ditches, I wondered?

"No, why?" I replied. "You are not worried about making this landing are you?"

He then said that he thought he could handle it alright but was just wanting to give me the option because, although he knew the correct drill for making a crash landing, he had never actually done one before. Certainly crash landings were fairly commonplace in the wartime RAF but, like Geoff, most pilots attempting one would be doing it for the first time. It was a matter of putting theory into practice – with only one chance of getting it right. However, I had faith in Geoff and there was no way that I would bale out and leave him to it. By the time we completed our circuit and he started his approach it was 0955 hours and I noted that we had been airborne for five hours and ten minutes.

As we neared the ground I was conscious that our speed was appreciably faster than normal because we had no flaps. Indeed, just before we touched down the ground seemed to be really whizzing past below, but perhaps this was also partly because I was about four feet nearer to it than during a normal landing. Everything now depended on Geoff. I felt helpless, knowing that I had no control over what would happen in the next few seconds.

I felt a slight bump as the tailwheel, which was a fixed one, touched first and then the front made contact, with hardly a bounce, as the whole aircraft slithered along the flat, grassy ground. Of course, I was jolted and bumped about a bit and there was much noise and juddering as the propeller blades were bent and forced to a halt. This would all have been a bit frightening had I not experienced the crash at Crosby-on-Eden the previous February. That had been much worse. By the time we slithered to a standstill, a few seconds later, Geoff had switched off the ignition and fuel valves. We both jumped out. It was a textbook 'belly flop', to use the RAF jargon. How wonderful it felt to have both feet firmly on the ground. We stood there, jubilant that we had done it and were safe.

Within seconds we were surrounded by ground staff. Members of the crash crew stood by the engines with foam extinguishers but they were not needed. Everyone crowded round Geoff, congratulating him on making a good job of the landing. I was standing behind the port wing when someone came up to me, shook my hand and said, "Gosh, you were lucky weren't you?" I started to make some complimentary remark about Geoff's skill when he interrupted. "No, not the landing, I mean *that!*" he said, pointing behind me. I turned and got the shock of my life as I saw a gaping hole in the side of the fuselage. It was some twelve inches in diameter without its turned, jagged edges and about eighteen inches directly below where I had been sitting.

Incredible though it may seem, I had forgotten, for the moment, the very reason why we had had to make the crash landing in the first place. The dramatic events at Letpedan flooded back into my mind. That ineffable 'half out of body' feeling must have been a cognition of the nearness of my death and not directly connected with the traumatic few seconds that followed, when I became convinced that Geoff had been killed and we were plunging into the ground.

However, I quickly resumed an air of nonchalance as others gathered round to examine the damage. On the other side of the fuselage there was a smaller, cleaner hole where the shell, which they reckoned must have been of 75mm calibre, had entered. If the shell had been about eighteen inches higher, it would most likely have removed the centre portion of my body with almost surgical precision. If it had been about eighteen inches further forward it would have severed my legs and worse – if there could be worse – it might have hit the magazines of our cannons and blown the Beaufighter in two. It had been a miraculous escape.

We were then whisked off for debriefing, which did not take long. It had not been a fruitful trip, but in war even the negative information that there were no signs of military activity in the area might have been useful. At least we had the satisfaction of watching them add another coloured dot to their 'flak map'!

By the time I got back to my hut and had changed out of my flying gear, I noticed that it was still only 1030 hours. Hunger suddenly made me remember that on the previous evening I had ordered a late breakfast for around this time. I wandered off towards the Mess. Although it would probably be the inevitable tasteless Soyalink sausages, a piece of bread fried in horrible *ghee* and a mug of tea tasting strongly of chlorine, I knew that on this particular morning it was going to taste *good!*

11.   Arrival at Chiringa

The very next day after our crash landing at Feni it was announced that the squadron would be moving to Chiringa, a forward landing strip about 90 miles further south down the coast near Cox's Bazaar. This move had been impending for a while, and advance parties of ground staff had already gone to make ready the site, which was currently not occupied. This should have been a rest day for us, but instead we were detailed to fly one of the Beaufighters to this new base.

My pals, Tubby and China, had gone on leave and China had entrusted me to look after one of his treasured possessions, a rather ancient wind-up gramophone and a case of classical records. These were too vulnerable to be sent by road, so I had to find room for them, together with my own kit, in the rear cockpit of the aircraft. The fuselage was already packed with other items of squadron equipment that were needed in advance of the main road convoy.

It was raining as we took off at 1510 hours in Beaufighter NE.713 Z for the 35-minute flight down to Chiringa and it was raining as we circled, under low cloud, to make our landing. The runway was easy to spot because it nestled neatly in a pronounced 'U' bend in the Matamuhari river, situated about 12 miles inland on the flat, low-lying coastal plain of the Arakan and about two miles west of the village of Chiringa, through which ran the only road in the vicinity, apart from a few tracks. The surrounding terrain was rather featureless scrubland, paddy fields, and some patches of woodland.

It was raining as we landed, in rather poor visibility and without any instructions from the ground. We had been warned that there was no R/T communication but we were surprised to find that there was not even anyone with an Aldis lamp manning the small Flying Control hut. We landed into what was nominally the prevailing wind. There was a windsock but it was hanging, or perhaps it would be more correct to say drooping, vertically downwards! The rain was falling gently but persistently straight down. Geoff made a good landing but I immediately noticed the difference in wheel noise compared with what we were used to at Feni, where the runway was surfaced with interlocking steel plates. Here, I found out later, the runway was surfaced with heavy canvas material, impregnated with Bitumen, laid over compacted earth, cambered like a road to facilitate drainage. The place looked deserted, but when we got to the end of the runway someone appeared and guided us to a dispersal area. Here there were perforated steel plates over the mud, which was just as well, otherwise we would probably have sunk up to our nacelles. Transport was in short supply and we had to wait some time, sheltering in the aircraft, before someone came to take us and our kit to our new living quarters.

It was raining as I struggled, carrying parachute, navigator's holdall, kitbag, suitcase, etc – and, of course, that precious gramophone – through a slippery sea of mud to the shelter of the first empty *basha* I could find. This was my first introduction to Chiringa, which was to be our new home for the next few monsoon months, and I was not impressed.

It rained more or less continuously for the next three or four days. This delayed some of the road transport and much of the equipment had not arrived. A small wooden bridge, just before the road reached Chiringa, had partly collapsed and some of the vehicles in the main convoy had to divert to Cox's Bazaar and wait there until it was repaired. Even the oft-used RAF expression 'organised chaos' was inadequate to describe the state of the place. A skeleton cookhouse staff produced meals of a sort, but there was, as yet, no cutlery or plates. I had to dig deep into the bottom of my kitbag to find 'knife, fork, spoon – airman for the use of' and a metal canteen, none of which had seen the light of day since I was a humble LAC at Initial Training Wing.

We all had to lend a hand unloading trucks and manhandling crates and other heavy pieces of equipment across the quagmire. I remember one day a gang of us crossed the river, a few at a time in a small boat, to the other bank where a large generator had been manhandled from the road to the water's edge. Our job was to help push it onto a wooden pontoon to float it a few yards to our bank. It was a terrible job pushing and shoving in the slippery mud, but this sort of activity engendered a feeling of camaraderie between all ranks, more akin to that which had existed at Bhatpara, but which had tended to be lacking at Feni where the site had been so spread out.

We got wet through but the only good thing was that it was not cold. The rain was tepid and the air mild for most of the time. Occasionally, there would be heavy downpours, lasting an hour or so, when a driving wind would spring up and send everyone scurrying for whatever shelter could be found. At night, I would retire to my rather isolated hut, which was only temporary accommodation, and in the flickering light of a hurricane lamp I would play some of China's gramophone records. My favourite was Beethoven's 6th Symphony which I played over and over again so that even today, although I am not a musical person, I can remember almost every note.

It was a depressing time but I thought at least there would be several more days respite from operations, but I was wrong. There had already been mutterings from Wing headquarters about the length of time it was taking for the squadron to get operational again and after five days, when things were still far from being properly organised on the ground, Geoff and I were briefed for a trip the next day. A slight improvement in the weather had been forecast but I was apprehensive about this trip.

I had studied my maps and realised that it was going to be a bit trickier operating from Chiringa in bad weather. From Feni there had been a greater distance in which to climb slowly before reaching the highest peaks of the Chin Hills and time to spot gaps in the clouds and make detours round the worst of the towering cumulonimbus that formed over these mountains at this time of year. Here at Chiringa we were much closer to the highest parts of the range. To set off in any direction between north east and south east it would be necessary to climb like the clappers immediately after take-off. Within about eight minutes we would have to clear foothills with peaks of around 2,700 feet. Thereafter, the hilltops would rise quite quickly and after only about twenty-five minutes the highest part of the range, with four peaks of 9,009, 8,244, 9,228 and 10,018 feet, would be strung out across our path. The latter peak, Mount Victoria, presented an additional hazard in that it was highly magnetic and could play havoc with the aircraft's magnetic compass. This was definitely not a good area to be flying in cloud.

Next morning the weather did not look much better to me. It was misty and drizzling. Nevertheless, I was ready and clad in my flying gear when Geoff came to collect me and we were driven out to the aircraft. Because of serviceability problems we were having to take one of 'A' Flight's aircraft, LX.938 D, which, for some reason, I never liked doing. We had actually started the engines but Geoff had to stop them again because there was a problem with the intercom. This often happened under these conditions of high humidity, usually due to condensation in the sockets into which the jack plugs had to be inserted. There was a delay of nearly an hour whilst the electrician got it working, but meanwhile visibility had become worse and Geoff decided to postpone take-off for a couple of hours.

I was taken back to my hut to wait. To fill in time I decided to play the gramophone and selected a record at random. It was 'Danse Macabre', hardly a good omen, I thought, but nevertheless I listened to it, with a strange fascination, right through – twice. I was getting more and more uptight about this trip as time dragged by. Eventually, after nearly three hours, Geoff came back in the jeep with two of the ground crew and said it had been decided that we should go.

It had stopped raining as we boarded the aircraft and visibility had certainly improved. We could see the full length of the runway as we taxied out and took off at 1345 hours. Geoff turned on to the heading I had given him and we began climbing. After a few fleeting glimpses of the ground we were in cloud. We had hoped that we would break through above this stratus cloud before reaching the highest ranges of the mountains but after about twenty minutes this was beginning to look increasingly unlikely. We were at about 7,000 feet and still flying in continuous cloud, and furthermore we were now experiencing considerable turbulence. This indicated that we were in cumulus or more likely cumulonimbus cloud. Geoff decided that it would be too risky to carry on and attempt to cross the mountains under these conditions, so we turned back.

Descending at a cautiously low rate, we broke through the cloud base about a couple of miles north of the runway and made a safe landing, after having been airborne for only one hour. That our first attempt at operations from this disorganised new base had been abortive was about the worst thing that could have happened. That evening, after yet another makeshift meal, I went to my hut, alone and in a slough of despond.

Next morning, however, Geoff came to see me with some good news. We were to go on leave! This was something I had hardly thought about, but seemingly the policy was, subject to operational requirements, that aircrew should have fourteen days leave every three months. We were just about due and Geoff's buddy Steve and his navigator Sammy, whom I knew and liked, were also due. The O/C of 'B' Flight had decided that we could all go together. Of course, there was nowhere suitable to go in the Arakan and it was the semi-official practice to fly aircrew to Calcutta in a Beaufighter. Such trips were logged in the Flight office records as 'extended air test'. I spent some time that day finding someone I could trust to look after the gramophone. At that time I did not have a small suitcase and I had to borrow one.

It was W/O England who was to fly us and we had to squeeze like sardines into the confined space of the Beaufighter's fuselage. This was the first of several such journeys I made and they were scary. Unlike the crew, we had no parachutes, lifejackets or dinghies. Although the trip would only take about an hour, part of it was over the shark-infested waters of the Bay of Bengal. The thought of having to ditch was too awful to contemplate, but the alternative was a 30-mile lift in a three-ton truck over a very bumpy road to Dohazari, where the railway started; a 120-mile journey via Chittagong and Feni to Chandpur in a packed, smelly train with cockroaches for company; a 60-mile trip on an ancient river steamer up the Ganges to Faridpur; then a 150-mile journey in another packed, smelly train down to Calcutta. You would arrive exhausted after this nightmare of a journey, which could take anything up to 48 hours. This is why we gratefully crawled into the fuselage!

In a little more than an hour, W/O England landed us at Dum Dum, one of two airfields at Calcutta. By early afternoon we were having drinks in Firpo's and planning our next day's journey up to Darjeeling.

This leave in Darjeeling would be a new experience for all of us – but that is another story.

Inside the Basha at Chiringa.

12. Ditching Imminent?

On a scale of one to ten, I would rate my swimming ability somewhere between nought and one! I have always been a bit afraid of the water, probably because I never had any proper swimming lessons as a young child. It was not until the age of fourteen, when I was at Leyton Technical College, that I went to a swimming bath for the first time. The Master in charge was not a qualified instructor but nevertheless I did learn how to tread water and to swim a short distance, using the breast stroke. But after a few sessions I decided that I definitely did not like being in the water and opted for the lesser evil of playing football, which was the only alternative offered to us on our so-called weekly 'sports' afternoons.

Thus, when I volunteered to join the RAF, I was a bit worried because I had heard that aircrew were supposed to be able to swim, although nobody said anything to me about it to begin with. Soon after induction, our course, numbering about thirty trainees, was sent to No.1 Initial Training Wing at Babbacombe, where our Sergeant was a small, athletic rugby playing Welshman named Lewis. In between lectures, he took us for drill, P.T. and lots of cross-county runs. It was early summer and we wore P.T. kit for running. He would jog along behind, shouting directional commands.

One day we were returning from a cross-country run and had reached the promenade at Babbacombe, which would take us back to the hotel where we were billeted but, unexpectedly, he directed us down a narrow, winding lane that led to the beach. There was a small stone jetty jutting out into the sea and as the leaders of the group drew level with it Sergeant Lewis again unexpectedly shouted, "Right wheel!"

Obediently, the group turned and trotted along the jetty but as the leaders got near the end they slowed down and some began to mark time, obviously expecting the order 'halt' or 'about turn'. But instead, Sergeant Lewis barked, "I didn't tell you to stop! Jump off and swim back to the beach!"

There was confusion and hesitation at the front but then they began jumping. To anyone watching it must have looked like a comic film, but I wasn't laughing – I was panic stricken. Would I be able to jump off? How deep was the water? But before I had time to think, the momentum of the still jogging group, which I was in the midst of, brought me to the brink. There was nothing for it but to jump, so I did.

I surfaced, spluttering, and started swimming laboriously towards the beach, using the breaststroke. Others seemed to be flashing past me, doing skilfully executed crawls, whilst I was hardly moving. From water level, the expanse of sea to the beach looked vast. I thought I would never make it without becoming exhausted. But then I realised that the water was becoming shallower very quickly, a fact of which Sergeant Lewis would have been well aware. A few more strokes and I found that my foot could touch the seabed. I was then able to wade, as indeed the others were now doing, for the remaining distance. We reached the beach and continued to jog along it, in dripping wet P.T. kit, towards our billet.

That had been rather a traumatic experience for me but I had made it and was beginning to feel pleased with myself, particularly as I looked back and saw that three of the group had refused to jump and were walking back from the jetty with Sergeant Lewis, who was no doubt giving them a wigging. This incident was the RAF's way, or more specifically Sergeant Lewis's way, of sorting out the swimmers from the non-swimmers!

In due course we moved on to No.1 Signals School at Cranwell for our training as wireless operators. In between lectures we sometimes had talks and demonstrations, such as how to put on our parachute harnesses and lifejackets correctly and how to fall onto the ground safely after parachuting, so it did not seem unusual that one day we were told to assemble after lunch near the main gate, where a coach would be taking us to a venue for a talk on ditching and survival procedures in dinghies. Not unusual, that is, until our instructor added, "Oh, by the way... bring your towels with you." *Towels? Surely we are not going to get wet,* I thought, *or he would have said to bring swimming trunks or P.T. shorts as well?* But I was wrong. The coach took us to a public swimming baths in a nearby town. These baths were, apparently, commandeered on occasions by the RAF. Certainly, we did have a talk about survival in dinghies, etc, but the real purpose of the visit was soon revealed. We were to have a swimming test. We were instructed to undress and put on blue battle dress and flying boots, selected from a pile of old uniforms obviously stored there for the purpose. As I got ready, I was filled with apprehension as I learned that we were to jump in at the deep end, kick off the flying boots, swim the length of the baths and climb, unaided, into a large rubber dinghy, which was tethered at the shallow end. All this without the Mae West lifejacket which aircrew normally wore.

But there was worse to come... We were not just to jump from the edge of bath but from the top diving board.

I was terrified!

When my turn came, my legs felt heavy as lead as, somehow, I managed to drag myself up what seemed like dozens of steps right to the top. This was the first time I had ever stood on a high diving board. I was aghast at how far down the water looked and indeed how small the pool appeared to be. As the Instructor shouted 'jump!' it was like a bad dream and as I fell I half expected to wake up. I did, with an almighty splash! Down I went, holding my breath in a mass of white water and bubbles for what seemed like ages. Eventually I surfaced, gasping, and instinctively tried to tread water. Almost automatically this led to my freeing first one foot and then the other of those boots. This had been easier than I had expected.

I started swimming laboriously towards the dinghy but soon found that wearing a wet uniform, and the fact that this was fresh water, made it much more exhausting than my previous experience in the sea at Babbacombe. Somehow, I reached the dinghy but by this time I was so exhausted that I couldn't climb aboard. There were three people already in it and on my third attempt one of my pals surreptitiously gave me a helping hand at a moment when the instructors attention was momentarily elsewhere. When I recovered, I felt greatly relieved. I had (with a little help from my friends!) passed the RAF's test and, as far as they were concerned, I was a 'swimmer'.

This had been my worst experience in training so far but at least it had given me a bit of confidence that if it came to the crunch, and I had to get out of a ditched plane and into a dinghy, I would be able to do it. During my subsequent flying training, which included quite a few trips over the sea, I was no longer bothered overmuch about my fear of water or my poor swimming ability. That is, until one day, while on operations in a Beaufighter, ditching really appeared to be imminent.

On 16th August 1944 we took off from Chiringa at 1055 hours in NE.752 X, together with five other aircraft, to attack shipping in the Gulf of Martaban. If no shipping was found we were to patrol the road/rail links between Moulmien and Kyaito, on the far side of the Gulf, which would be at about the limit of our range. F/O Cuddy was leading as we set off in a loose echelon formation down the coast along the Naf peninsula. We were last in line, with Steve and Sammy in front of us. As we left the tip of the peninsula, we reduced height to about 200 feet over the sea as we headed for Oyster Island.

Oyster Island, which lay about 13 miles off the coastline, had to be seen to be believed. It was a tiny island, looking like a sandbank. It was only about 700 feet long by 80 feet across at the widest point, yet it had 27 palm trees on it. In amongst the trees there were several bamboo Bashas and store buildings. It was exactly what most people would imagine a desert island to be like, except for one feature – in the middle of it was a full size lighthouse. It marked the northern end of a dangerous reef, which lay under the surface, roughly parallel to the coast, almost to the mouth of the Kaladan river, where Japanese-occupied Akyab harbour was situated. The lighthouse was not in operation nor was the island occupied by the Japanese. Whilst it made a good observation post, it was simply too small, too close to the coast and too vulnerable to attack to be held by either side. There were rumours of clandestine visits by the Japanese, who set booby traps, followed by equally clandestine visits by Allied forces, who booby trapped the booby traps! However, even if there was no boat visible at the little wooden jetty, you could never be sure that there were no concealed Japanese machine gunners on the island, so it was best not to fly too close.

On this occasion, still flying low over the sea, we skirted it about two miles on the seaward side. F/O Cuddy, our leader, altered course a few degrees to port onto a heading that would take us all the way over the water for about 206 miles until we converged with the coastline at Bawmi Bay. Here we would turn inland and fly across the Bassien delta to get to the Gulf of Martaban. Since we were just following the others, I had little to do and was sitting with my swivel seat facing backwards, keeping lookout.

Although we were well into the monsoon period the weather was calm but dull. The sky was heavily overcast, which made the sea look grey and, I thought, menacing. Geoff and I had already done several trips down this coastal route and were familiar with it. As we flew on, I recalled a weird experience we had on one of these trips when we had been flying alone along this same part of the Bay of Bengal. It had been a 'grey day' similar to this but when the sea was even more calm and glassy in appearance.

From our training days in Canada, Geoff was well aware of the danger of misjudging height when low flying over such seas, as altimeters could not be relied upon below about 150 feet, yet, oddly, he suddenly said to me, "What height do you reckon we are flying at Denny?"

I looked over the side of my cupola and was about to say between 200 and 300 feet when, to my astonishment, the sea seemed to 'jump up' to a higher level. I was so taken-aback by this illusion that I delayed answering for a few seconds until I had taken another careful look and made a judgement.

"Between 50 and 100 feet," I said. "But why are you asking?"

"Well," he replied, "a short while ago I thought I was at least 200 feet but then the sea seemed to jump up. It must have been an illusion."

When I then told him that I too had just experienced the same illusion we were both amazed. I knew from having studied the physics of light at technical college that this illusion was possible under 'millpond' surface conditions but had always regarded it as a rather subjective phenomenon. However, for us both to have experienced the illusion at the same time seemed to challenge this belief. We discussed it for a few minutes and Geoff said it stressed the importance of us both being vigilant at all times when low flying over sea as well as land.

Fortunately, today there was a slight breeze, causing little ripples on the sea and Geoff had four other aircraft in front of him, which made it easier to judge height. We flew on in silence until we were about two thirds of the way to Bawmi Bay, when Geoff said, "I'm a bit worried about the port engine. There seems to be a bit of vibration. Can you feel it?" Being a worrier myself, I was usually the first to notice any abnormality in engine noises but up to that moment both engines had sounded O.K. to me and I told him so. He didn't sound too concerned and we carried on.

At about 1240 hours, we were just approaching the coast at Bawmi Bay when I too felt some vibration on that port engine, which seemed to come on quite suddenly. I was about to tell Geoff but I didn't need to.

"That port engine is bad, Denny," he said with some concern. "I'm going to turn back. What course do I steer?"

"Three three zero," I replied, which would head us back initially to Foul Island. He started a steep turn to starboard, breaking away from the other four, who continued on across the land. They would be flying across the delta, where it was advisable to maintain strict R/T silence, because of the proximity of Bassien and Mingladon, both of which had airstrips where there might be enemy fighters. Nevertheless, we had hardly completed our turn when I heard Steve say, "Are you in trouble Vardi?" Transmissions over enemy territory were usually clipped like this, without call signs.

"Yes, port engine, may have to ditch," replied Geoff.

Geoff was not one to use words lightly and, in any case, the tone of his voice left me in no doubt that he meant what he said. I felt a wave of panic as the possibility of ditching, which one tended to think of as something that only happened to others, was suddenly an imminent reality. Then, as though seeking re-assurance, my mind flashed back to that time at the swimming baths when I had jumped off the high diving board. This would not be so bad, I thought. This time I was wearing my Mae West, my dinghy was clipped to my parachute harness and there would be no distance to swim, and my boots...? That was when I felt a second wave of panic! This time I was wearing laced-up marching boots, which could not be removed so easily as the normal fur-lined suede flying boots I had been wearing at the baths. Should I take them off before we ditched? But I might need them if we later made it to land...

I was still trying to make up my mind as to what was the best thing to do when I was distracted by a crackle on the R/T and a faint voice, probably F/O Cuddy, saying what may have been, "Go with them Steve". I don't think Geoff heard this, as his attention was taken up with other things.

First, he warned me that he was going to jettison the rockets. He fired all eight in one salvo and I watched the splashes in the sea ahead of us. We were about 250 miles from base, still with more than half our maximum weight of fuel on board. There was no provision for jettisoning part of this and if we lost the port engine it was very doubtful whether we would be able to maintain height on one engine. Then he began tinkering with the controls, throttling the engine back a bit to a point where the vibration lessened. For the moment it was still running, albeit at reduced power.

I took a look around to make sure that there were no enemy fighters in the vicinity but saw nothing except another Beaufighter, about three miles behind us. Obviously, Steve had indeed turned round to escort us and I told Geoff. Neither he nor Steve would want to risk having any unnecessary R/T conversation so close to the enemy coast and silence was maintained. Whilst it felt reassuring to know they were there, they could do nothing to help us except, in event of us ditching, note our exact position and whether we had got out of the aircraft. They would then carry on back to base and report it. Only with such positive information would any air sea rescue attempt be made, although at the moment we were too far south for this to be practical.

Ahead I could see Foul Island, which we would reach in a few minutes. Foul Island was of volcanic origin and rose starkly out of the sea, about twenty miles off the coast, a semi-spherical rock about two miles in diameter and covered with green growth. It must have been a wonderful haven for seabirds, but was otherwise uninhabited. At some points, the rock face was almost vertical at sea level but there were other places where little rocky beaches would make landing by dinghy possible. We had been told that there was a cache of emergency rations and medicines buried on the island at a place where there were several graves of allied personnel. The cache was said to be buried in a grave marked P/O Prune. Presumably, this was intended to fool the Japanese, who would not know that P/O Prune was a fictitious character who appeared in articles in an aircrew training manual as a clot who was always doing the wrong thing. I was desperately trying to remember what I had been told about this. Was it true and on which side of the island were the graves?

Geoff and I discussed what we should do. If ditching was inevitable, it would be better to put down beside Foul Island and get on shore. If Steve reported that we had done this, then there was a remote possibility of being rescued by launch. But now that Geoff had reduced the revs on the port engine it was still running and we were maintaining height, albeit at reduced airspeed. The island was now just about three minutes flying away and Geoff had to make a decision.

He decided to fly on. We passed the island about two miles on the seaward side and I watched it slip slowly away behind us. The next twenty minutes was a nail-biting time, but gradually our confidence grew. The engine seemed to have stabilised, we were maintaining height, our airspeed was 165 knots and Steve was trailing behind us. There still had been no R/T conversation between Geoff and Steve, which was just as well, as we were now approaching the next danger point, the offshore island of Cheduba. Cheduba was occupied by Japanese troops and had ack-ack defences. There was clear water, the Cheduba Straits, between it and the larger offshore island of Ramree, which was closer to the mainland. But we decided that it would be safer to keep over the open sea on the west side of Cheduba. We skirted it without incident and ahead was now 100 miles of open sea to Oyster Island. It did occur to me that midway we would be about 30 miles from any point on land but somehow I knew that we would now make it back to base. In any case, the lie of the land was such that I could now send an SOS by W/T myself, if need be.

Time dragged on until, at 1400 hours, we reached Oyster Island, making a slight alteration of course, which brought us to the tip of the Naf peninsular about ten minutes later. We would now be flying up 'friendly' coastline and at this point Steve broke R/T silence, saying, "Will you be alright now Vardi? I am going to get rid of my RPs."

"Yes," Geoff replied, "I think we'll be OK now thanks."

I watched Steve break away and turn southward. We learned later that he had doubled back to Akyab and fired his whole salvo of RP into the jetty and buildings at the harbour, evidently taking the Japanese completely by surprise.

We carried on to Chiringa, where we landed without incident at 1445 hours. It had been a memorable trip for me. I, with my fear of the water, had actually experienced what it felt like to know that ditching was imminent. But it hadn't happened. In some strange way, this lessened my worries about flying down that coast over the Bay of Bengal again, which I subsequently had to do five more times.

13. Marathon Trips

Prequel

When I returned from leave in mid-October, life at Chiringa was undergoing change. Now that 177 Squadron was also here and was operational, the place was getting busier. The small flying control building was now being manned continuously by personnel trained in air traffic control instead of by off-duty aircrew. Because the aircraft dispersal points for the two squadrons were widely separated, the single airstrip was used for take-offs and landings in both directions when the wind was light. This was to avoid an aircraft having to taxi the full length of the strip and turn about to take-off 'into wind'. There were, of course, no hard surfaced taxi tracks.

There was not a great deal of fraternisation with aircrews of 177 Squadron, who occupied a separate camp and had their own Messes. There had been some talk of combining resources and having common Messing facilities but not everyone was in favour. It was even rumoured that 27 Squadron, who were becoming operational again, might also be moving here, to form what would become 901 Beaufighter Wing.

I was still sharing the same room with Tubby, China and Hoppy. Our basha was on the edge of the camp. Behind it was some grassland and then some trees that marked the line of the only road in the vicinity which, so far as we were concerned, ran from nowhere to nowhere. It was a quiet corner to relax in when not flying. Tubby had a galvanised steel bath (a highly-prized possession, of which there were very few in the camp) which he allowed us to use and China had a clockwork gramophone (also a rarity) and some light classical records, which we would often listen to sitting on the veranda in the late afternoon or at dusk, before going to dinner in the Mess. This had been our home for three months and life was beginning to develop some sort of pattern.

Bathtime at Chiringa.

The war situation was changing also. Throughout the whole monsoon period, which was now nearing its end, our squadron had been operating almost every day without any stand-downs. Sorties had been mainly to the central area of Burma but the seeming effectiveness of the interdiction policy was forcing the Japanese to use transportation mainly under cover of darkness. Fewer targets were being found in the central areas and daylight sorties were now being extended to targets even further east and to the very limits of the Beaufighter's range.

Both squadrons were increasingly undertaking shipping strikes and reconnaissance along the eastern side of the Gulf of Martaban around Moulmein – patrols along the railway from Moulmein to Kaikto and Pegu – and more recently, sorties right across central Burma into Siam and across to the Lampang-to-Changrai road. The first two areas could be reached by flying down the Burmese coast, a few miles offshore, to Gwa Bay and then cutting across land a comparatively short distance to the Gulf. Flying over the sea was less of a strain for the pilot. One could fly straight and level and there was no need to keep too low. To get to the Changrai road, however, there was no alternative but to fly right across central Burma, at low-level most of the way, and climb up again onto the plateau crossing Siam.

I thought of these as 'marathon' flights. It took about three hours to get to the Changrai road, where any patrol would be limited to not more than thirty minutes in order to have sufficient fuel for a further three-hour flight back to base.

Returning from leave and having to resume operational flights, with all the dangers involved, was depressing enough, but unsettling changes and the knowledge that sorties were tending to become longer and more dicey made it even more depressing. A tour of operations was 300 flying hours and to date I had done about 180. There had been continual losses at about the rate of one crew every two weeks in 'B' Flight (and about the same in 'A' Flight) and one could only look ahead with apprehension. Would we survive and what would the last trip be like?

Because the squadron, with its present personnel, had only been formed and started operating at the beginning of the year, it was an inescapable fact, lurking in the back of my mind, if I ever dared to think about it, that *no crew had yet completed a tour.*

This was the situation when Geoff and I resumed operations but shortly afterwards, at about the end of October, what seemed to me like a miracle occurred. It was announced, without much ado, that a tour of operations in this theatre was now only 200 hours. There were feelings of elation all round. On 'B' Flight S/L Muller-Rowlands, who was our acting CO, had already completed more than 200 hours and, as this was his second tour, he was due for immediate repatriation to the UK. Steve and Sammy now had only a few hours to do, and then, if our luck held out, Geoff and I would be next to finish, with about 20 hours still to do.

But my feelings of elation became more subdued when I realised that, although we could now see light at the end of the tunnel, we still had to *get* to the end of the tunnel. Twenty hours would mean several trips each, with the same ever-present hazards.

Our next operation after the news that the length of a tour had now been reduced was, in fact, one of those marathon trips to the Changrai road. We were briefed on the afternoon of 9th November for a sortie the next day. Two aircraft from 'A' Flight were to go earlier in the morning and then Geoff and I, in aircraft NV.256 'Y', together with F/O Stayman and W/O Hopkins in NV.210 'W', would take-off later at 1015 hours, so as to arrive on patrol in the early afternoon. I had mixed feelings about this. On the one hand, it would be over six hours duration, which would bring our total hours that much nearer to the requirement for completion of our tour. On the other hand, it would be our first time to go to that remote area of Siam and would involve even longer than usual periods of low flying over land for Geoff. Also, it would be a mid-morning take-off. For long flights I much preferred pre-dawn take-offs, when we could traverse part of Burma before sunrise.

Duly, the next day, F/O Stayman and Hoppy took off at 1012 hours, followed by us about three minutes later. We did not intend to stay together because our tracks would soon diverge. They were aiming for Lampang at the south end and would patrol about half of it up to Bhayo, whereas we were aiming for Bhayo and would patrol the other half of the road up to the outskirts of Changrai. Indeed, by the time we had turned on to a heading of 119 degrees and started to climb we had lost sight of them.

On this heading we had to climb quite quickly to clear the rapidly rising wooded hilltops. The engines seemed to be labouring away, using fuel that we could ill spare, but there was no way of avoiding this. We had to get to at least 9,000 feet in about 25 minutes to clear the high ground a few miles south of mount Victoria, where our track was taking us. The peak of this mountain was a hazard to navigation, not just because it was 10,000 feet high but also because it contained magnetic ore, which could play havoc with the normal aircraft compass. But Geoff had taken the precaution of re-setting our gyro compass some ten minutes previously and was steering by this. It was just as well he had done so, because he mentioned that he had observed a noticeable deflection on the needle of our magnetic compass as we drew level and passed the mountain, even though we were several miles distant from it.

A few minutes later, the successive ridges of mountains began to reduce in height quite quickly. Geoff put the nose down and we descended rapidly, at times losing more than 1,000 feet a minute. The effect was the discomfort of suddenly getting hotter and experiencing the almost oppressive sickly smell of vegetation. I used to think of this as 'the smell of Burma'. After a short while, we would cease to notice it as we were immersed in it all the time. We hugged the treetops as much as possible, to lessen the chance of being spotted by any observation posts in the foothills, but this added to our discomfort because of considerable bumpiness caused by thermal currents. It was a relief to get down to relatively level ground and to resume our normal cruising speed of 180 knots.

Our track would take us across the Irrawaddy at a point where a tributary, the Kyaw, flowed into it. On the far bank was the town of Chauk, which had a number of oil well installations; these were quite heavily defended by both heavy and medium anti-aircraft guns. Also in that area were rapid-firing 30mm cannon and machine guns, deployed along the riverbank for defence against low-flying aircraft like ourselves. Therefore, before reaching the river, we made a small detour and crossed it at a point about seven miles south of Chauk. Geoff weaved violently as we skimmed across the water but we were not fired upon.

We resumed our intended track and pressed on across the central part of Burma. This was familiar territory, where we had made a number of sorties in the past, but today it felt different. We had crossed a railway and several roads. Normally we would take a good look in both directions as far as we could see. Geoff always looked to the left and I to the right, searching for any telltale signs of rising dust or smoke that might indicate road or rail traffic on the move, which we would go and investigate. But today we glanced briefly, knowing that if we did spot anything we could ill afford the fuel to make any detours. Our immediate task was to get from one side of Burma to the other.

In due course we crossed a second railway with a road running alongside it, about three miles north of Yamethin. I remembered that on a previous occasion we had been hit by machine gun fire along this stretch but today no one fired at us and nothing was seen. We were now approaching unfamiliar territory. Ahead we could see the land rising up, not so much as a range of hills but more of a plateau, where, according to my map, the general height of the land would be 5,000 to 6,000 feet from now on.

The land was now becoming thickly wooded and with fewer signs of habitation. We had started to increase height early, so our rate of climb would not be too great and thereby economise on fuel. As I noted down the time and we began our climb, the 'marathon' nature of this flight seemed to strike me. *We had been airborne for an hour and twenty minutes and yet we were barely half way to Bhayo, where our patrol would begin!*

We had nearly reached 6,000 feet when a slight movement on the ground caught my eye. I turned my head and looked out on the starboard quarter. I saw a small convoy of four camouflaged military vehicles driving along a road, little more than a track, which emerged from a valley descending from the high ground. They were now crossing flat, open scrubland and driving quite fast in the direction of Yamathin. Although from our height and distance they looked like Dinky toys, I estimated that they were at least 3-tonners. They were canvas-topped and the flaps at the backs were closed. Nobody appeared to be looking out at the rear.

I told Geoff, who immediately banked a bit and turned to starboard so that he could get a look. "Damn," he said. I didn't have to ask him what he meant. He was faced with a dilemma. If he continued his turn and descended rapidly back, skimming the treetops down the hillside, he could attack them from behind, probably taking them completely by surprise. One long burst of cannon fire would no doubt set all four ablaze in one attack, but we both knew that if he did this we would have to abandon the sortie we had been briefed to make. We simply didn't have enough fuel margin to make the long climb back up onto the plateau again, proceed to Bhayo, do our thirty minute patrol, fly back all the way across Burma again and then another climb up to 9,000 feet to get back over the Chin Hills.

After a couple of minutes discussion Geoff said, "What shall we do Denny?" Of course, it was up to him to decide, but he seemed to be leaving it to me!

There was no doubt in my mind that I wanted him to attack them, making two or three runs if necessary to ensure that they were completely destroyed, then we could return to base, perhaps finding some targets of opportunity on the way. But was this a soft option? Certainly, I was a bit apprehensive about carrying on with this long flight over unfamiliar territory, right to the limit of our range, not knowing what sort of opposition we might encounter. If we didn't carry on, what would we say at debriefing? The Wing Intelligence people did not mind if you attacked military targets on the way to or from a specified one, but they might not be too pleased if we had chosen to attack something else *instead* of carrying out the sortie as briefed. Perhaps it was with this in mind that I replied, reluctantly, "I think we should let them go and carry on to Bhayo."

"Yes, I think you're right," he said, as he resumed our course and began climbing again.

I was still facing backwards and watched these seemingly toy vehicles recede in a cloud of dust. At that moment, I felt I had acted like God. The drivers and any other personnel in them would never know that I had let them live.

Geoff had levelled out now at an altitude of around 6,000 feet above sea-level, although we were only about 200 feet above the treetops of this now thickly-wooded plateau terrain. He could relax a bit now. There was no need to fly lower, as this whole area was sparsely populated. We were still in Burma, but the Japanese would be pretty thin on the ground in this remote region.

The sky was blue, with a smattering of cumulus clouds, the sun was still high above and the panoramic views were fantastic. We had crossed over two or three north-to-south flowing rivers in ravine-like valleys, which had been quite impressive, but in due course I warned Geoff that we were coming up to the big one – the Salween.

Nevertheless, it still took us by surprise! One minute we were flying just above the treetops, then suddenly it was like flying off a sharp-edged cliff. For a few fleeting moments there was a breathtaking glimpse of this fast-flowing river, glistening in the sunshine about 2,000 feet below, in a deep ravine. Several patches of white water were visible, where small cataracts were formed by rocks. Then, in next to no time, wc were flying over treetops again, on the other side of the ravine, without a river in sight.

A few minutes later, we crossed the border and were now in Siam. The terrain was much the same but the general height of the land was becoming lower. One exception was the quite prominent mountain peak of Chiendago, just to the south, which my map indicated was 7,159 feet high. In the valley beyond this mountain was the only road in the area, which ran south to the major town of Chiengmai, about 35 miles distant. Chiengmai was a Japanese garrison town known to have anti-aircraft defences and also a landing strip where some fighter aircraft were kept. From here on, I had to keep a sharp lookout.

We flew on for another 15 minutes over a succession of ridges and valleys until finally, over one last small ridge, there lay a broad area of flat grassland. Soon we could see Bhayao and the road leading northward out of it. It was 1255 hours, in the heat of the afternoon, and it had taken us 2 hours and 40 minutes to get here. The town was quite small and although a few Japanese military vehicles may be sheltering there, they would be amongst civilians and we were not briefed to attack them. We were not at war with the Siamese. Our brief was to look for military vehicles on the move. We turned northward and began our patrol along the road.

It looked in good condition. I didn't know what the surface was but it was light ochre in colour, maybe crushed soft rock like sandstone. As far ahead as we could see, it was deserted. In fact, the whole area seemed to be deserted and idyllically peaceful in the bright sunshine. After about ten minutes Geoff said he could see something on the road ahead and when we reached it we saw that it was a steam road roller. It was clean and looked as though it had been recently painted. There were no people, nor any other mending equipment anywhere to be seen. It did not appear to be under steam, nor had it been recently attacked, because there were no marks on the ground. We could not see into its coal-bunker because there was something covering it, but if it had run out of fuel there were plenty of sources of wood nearby. We could only conclude that it had run out of water. It was very odd, but since we had been briefed that all forms of road-mending equipment were military targets, Geoff said we must attack it.

It had even occurred to us that it might be a decoy (the area close to the far side of it was thickly wooded and there could be machine gun posts) and Geoff asked me to keep a sharp lookout all round while he circled and made his attack. The ammunition in our 20mm cannons was mixed armour piercing, high-explosive and incendiary shells. Even so, it was difficult to observe what damage had been done to a sturdy machine like a steam roller and he made a second attack for good measure. There was no sign of any steam, water or oil, although there was quite a bit of fire and smoke from our incendiary rounds.

We then continued northwards up the road but it was deserted. At a point where it crossed a small river called Nam Me Lao, we were still about ten miles south of the town of Chiengrai. But our calculated time allotted for the patrol was up and, somewhat reluctantly, because we had not found any traffic on the road, we turned westward towards base. I looked backwards at the area we were leaving and had a still moment. The scene was so beautiful and peaceful in the afternoon sunshine, with a blue sky and a scattering of cumulus clouds, but looking northeast I could see rising hills in the distance, where the scene looked more ominous.

With a slight shiver, I recalled a general briefing that if we were in trouble in this area, for example if we had engine trouble or had used up too much fuel making a detour to avoid an enemy fighter, then rather than crash landing or baling out over Japanese-held territory, we should fly on in the direction I was looking as an 'escape' route. It was less than a hundred miles to the Chinese border. The Chinese were nominally Allies but had little interest in war with Japan in this remote area.

It would take us just over an hour to get back to the edge of the plateau and descend again to the central plain of Burma, but it was the first half hour that was dangerous, when there was a possibility of interception by fighters coming up from Changmai. This might well mean having to turn back, when heading off into the 'unknown' of semi-hostile China might become a reality, but we flew on for this first half hour without incident and the threat from fighters was now receding.

Because of the direction we had flown on the patrol, our homeward track was a bit further north and we came upon the Salween river sooner. Indeed, we followed its course for a little while, crisscrossing from one side to the other, fascinated by glimpses of that awesome river in the canyon below. Then, when the river took an almost ninety-degree bend to south, and almost at the point where we had crossed it on the outward journey, we left it and set course for home.

It was now easier for Geoff, as we could fly straight and level at a comfortable height of around 500 feet over the sparsely populated range of wooded hills in this part of Burma.

Time seemed to be dragging on a bit until we eventually reached the end of the plateau, near Nankwe again, and descended quite rapidly onto the central plain. We were near the point where we had seen those four vehicles. This prompted a discussion between Geoff and myself as to whether we would report seeing them. We decided it would be best not to. This would forestall any possible criticism that might be made by the Intelligence Officer (with the benefit of hindsight) that it would have been better to have destroyed four military vehicles than damage one steam road roller.

As we flashed across the railway and road just south of Yamethin we saw nothing in either direction. I kept thinking we were nearly home but we were still about an hour and twenty minutes from base. Furthermore, for the next thirty minutes Geoff, who had now been flying for about five hours and would be getting tired, would be low flying again and frequently having to weave as a precautionary measure as we passed near larger villages or groups of buildings.

Eventually we reached the Irrawaddy and crossed it without incident. It must have been a great relief to Geoff when, a few minutes later, we began the long climb over the mountains. It was mid-afternoon and there was quite a build-up of cumulus cloud above, but visibility was good below and between the clouds, so I had no problem keeping to our track. In due course we began to descend, as the hills got lower and lower and I heard Geoff mutter those welcome words, "OK, I can see it now." I was facing forward, the nose was down, and I could look along the top of the fuselage. I too could see it in the distance, the runway and groups of bashas nestling in a 'U' bend in that little Matamuhari river, which was 'home'. It was Chiringa!

Tired though he may have been, Geoff made a perfect landing at 1625 hours. We had been airborne for six hours and ten minutes. It had been a hell of a long way to go to attack a steam road roller!

14. Breakfast in the Officers' Mess

As on all RAF stations, 211 Squadron Officers' and NCOs ate, drank and socialised in their respective Messes at Chiringa. It was rare for NCOs to enter the Officers' Mess except by invitation on some special occasion. It was even more rare for an NCO to eat there, but on one occasion I did – and for the most unlikely meal – breakfast! I remember it, not only because it was an unusual experience but also because it was yet another occasion when Geoff showed his concern for me – his 'crew'.

On 26th September we were due to take off at 0530 hours in Beaufighter NE.210 'W', having been briefed the previous afternoon to do a shipping reconnaissance in the Gulf of Martaban, off the port of Moulmein. Also, we were given some leaflets to drop on villages in the Bassien delta on the way. Owing to a slight technical problem with the aircraft, we did not actually leave until 0615 hours.

The flight down the coast to Foul Island was uneventful. Here we turned towards the coast on a course of about 120° which would take us to Gwa Bay and then across the Delta to the Gulf of Martaban. The terrain across the Delta was a flat patchwork of paddy fields, marshes, wooded areas and small villages interconnected by a maze of little waterways. There were two main rivers, both navigable by biggish river steamers, the Bassien and the Irrawaddy with its multiplicity of outlets to the sea. There were very few roads and access to many of the small villages was by waterway, using sampans or other small vessels. There was one railway, between Bassien and Henzada, which ran diagonally across our path. We crossed this after about five minutes but saw nothing on it.

As we flew on, I dropped handfuls of leaflets out of the opening at the rear of my Cupola whenever we passed near or over any small villages. These were not leaflets in Japanese, intended for soldiers, which was what we usually dropped, but newssheets printed in Burmese. They were folded over to form a mini newspaper with four pages and diagrams, showing how the Allied Forces were advancing in Europe and other theatres of war.

While we flew on, I was keeping a nervous eye open on our port side, where Rangoon and its Mingladon airfield lay, about twenty miles distant. It was known that some Japanese fighter aircraft were based there, although at this time they were believed to be in short supply and they did not usually scramble them for only one intruding plane. Nevertheless, this was a dangerous area to be delivering newspapers!

A bit further on we passed over some paddy fields where women were planting rice. Obviously, they had not heard us coming until we 'whooshed' over them. I saw some look up, startled, and start to run, panic-stricken, to the cover of trees some distance away. It's not so easy to move quickly when you are almost knee-deep in muddy water and some of them fell over. I wanted to call out to them that we were not at war with the Burmese and did not wish to harm them. Many of these workers would be frightened to pick up the newsletters in case the Japanese caught them but I am sure that some would find their way into the villages and then, no doubtn word would spread about things the Japanese would rather the villagers didn't know.

Eventually we crossed the coastline about 10 miles west of Elephant Point and were now flying low over the sea again in the Gulf of Martaban, heading for Moulmien. This port was about 10 miles inland at a point where the Salween river splits into two deep-water channels, giving access to the sea for ocean-going vessels. Moulmien was heavily defended but our job was to patrol the sea between these two channels, with the hope of catching vessels entering or leaving.

We duly reached and patrolled the sea in the area between Amherst and the other outlet to the north of it but nothing was seen anywhere except near the tiny island of Bilugyun, where there were a few small fishing vessels. We left them in peace. After half an hour, which was the maximum we could allow due to fuel considerations, we turned back across the Gulf, heading for Elephant Point.

Half way across, I happened to be looking forward when, much to my consternation, I saw two little dots in the sky above Elephant Point. I drew Geoff's attention to them and we agreed that there was no doubt about it. They were two Japanese fighters, probably Oscars, patrolling the coastline at about 5,000 feet. More alarmingly, they were in the way of our route home.

The single-engined Oscar was faster and more manoeuvrable than the Beaufighter and to engage in aerial combat with one of them would most likely result in us being shot down. To engage with two would be suicidal. Furthermore, Geoff would have to open up the throttles to our maximum airspeed of around 210 knots and we were so far away from base that to fly at this speed for even 10 to 15 minutes would use so much fuel that we may not be able to get back.

We were about ten miles from the coast and flying low over the sea. I told Geoff that up to this point I was convinced that they had not seen us and he decided that the best thing to do would be to turn west towards the open sea and make a run for it.

This we did, flying along the south end of the Delta, trying to keep at least 10 miles out to sea. Meanwhile, I was looking backwards, keeping a very nervous eye on those fighters. For a while it was very scary, until I was relieved to see that they did not appear to be flying in our direction. In fact, they actually appeared to be circling Elephant Point as though they were waiting for us to return.

We had intended to fly right on to Pagoda Point before turning north to fly home but because we were getting worried about fuel consumption we now decided to risk taking a 'short cut' across the delta, inland behind Pagoda Point. We did not encounter any ack-ack fire but I was still keeping a sharp lookout for fighters and it was not until we got to the main ocean and made our way up to Foul Island that I felt I could begin to relax. From then on, the flight was uneventful and we landed back at Chiringa at about 1200 hours.

Debriefing did not take long, as we had not found any targets to attack but we did, of course, report the presence of the fighters. By the time I was dropped off at my basha I was both tired and hungry, having had nothing to eat that day but a piece of chocolate, but I suddenly remembered that the previous evening I had ordered a late breakfast, so with great anticipation I strode over to the Mess, still in my flying gear. The Mess was empty except for two ground staff NCOs, F/S (Lofty) Lambert and F/S (Sid) Teague, who were sitting chatting at a table, empty tea mugs in front of them. Lofty was a rather quiet but nice guy and was liked by the maintenance staff who were responsible to him. Sid, I had not had much to do with, but he also was very popular, particularly with the rank and file, but I don't think he had much time for aircrew. As Sid was the one in charge of the people in the cookhouse, I reminded him about my late breakfast.

With a 'you must be joking' attitude he reminded me that it had been ordered for 1030 hours. I hadn't arrived, so it had been thrown away, the cookhouse lads were now on a break, and I would have to wait until lunchtime before I could have anything to eat. I had forgotten that first our take-off had been delayed and then, of course, we'd had to make that detour because of those Japanese fighters and now, in fact, it was past noon.

After that long and, in parts, stressful flight even a corned beef sandwich would have been heaven but I was too tired to argue. I walked disconsolately out of the Mess and back to my basha, where I slumped on to my charpoy feeling tired beyond reason. I would have, no doubt, fallen asleep, still in my flying suit, but after about five minutes someone came to the open door. It was Geoff.

"I understand that you can't get anything to eat in your Mess," he said. "Come over to ours. There's still plenty of eggs, bacon and stuff left over from breakfast. I've spoken to the CMC and he says it's all right for you to come."

I was flabbergasted! What had happened was that Lofty, taken aback at Sid's 'couldn't care less' attitude, had telephoned Geoff in the Officer's Mess and told him that I was unable to get anything to eat. Geoff could have just said to send me over to the Officer's Mess but he knew me well enough to know that probably I wouldn't go, so he had actually left his Mess and walked the short distance to my Basha to take me back with him.

I was a bit reticent at first, because I was still in flying gear, but then I realised that so was Geoff, so I went back with him to his Mess. There were only a few people about as we sat down at a long table, where a bearer brought us each a large plate of eggs, bacon, sausages (the dreaded soya-links but on this occasion even these tasted good) and fried bread. There were three other officers at the table and they engaged in friendly chat. In no way did they make me feel that I was an interloper. When the meal was over I thanked them all, returned to my basha, climbed out of my flying gear and flopped onto my charpoy. Just before I sank into peaceful oblivion, my mind drifted back to that 'crewing up' meeting we had at No.32 OTU in Canada, back in the summer of 1943, when navigators and pilots chose each other by mutual agreement.

I think I chose a good 'un.

15. My Two 'Last' Trips

Of course, I know that there can't be two 'last' trips but in my case I feel that there were! The unexpected announcement, a few weeks beforehand, that in order to complete an operational tour, aircrews in the Far East would henceforth only be required to fly 200 operational hours rather than the 300 previously required, had been greeted with considerable relief. Three 211 Squadron crews had already exceeded the required total and were consequently tour-expired with immediate effect, which meant that they were also spared the anxiety of making that that fraught 'last trip', about which many of us were somewhat superstitious.

By 1st December I had completed just under 196 hours and we were due to fly the next day. On the way to the briefing room that afternoon I was thinking that this would probably be my penultimate trip, but when I found out where we were going I was taken aback to realise that it would, most probably, be our last, for it was to be another of those marathon trips into Siam, almost the same as the one we had made on 10th November, at the very limit of our range and over six hours in duration. Such a trip would almost certainly take my cumulative operational hours above the required total. I knew that Geoff's total to date was a bit less than mine (because I had done that trip with F/O Moffat when I first joined the squadron and was waiting for Geoff to arrive after his sick-leave) but a long trip like this would surely end his tour also.

We were to go to Bhayo, as before, but instead of patrolling the road up to Changrai, we were to cross it and to continue flying eastwards, over the next range of hills, to a small town called Maung Phoyao. From there, a minor road, little more than a track, also ran northwards to Changrai. Apparently, it was believed that the Japanese might be using it in daylight hours as an alternative to the main road. There wasn't much planning I needed to do, as the route would be the same as before, except for a little bit of unknown terrain at the limit of our range.

As I went over to the Mess for dinner that evening, my mind was in a whirl. I felt as though my last trip had been sprung on me without having had a couple of days to 'psyche myself up' for it. Of course, from an objective point of view there was no greater possibility of disaster striking on one's last trip than on any other, but subjectively there was a psychological barrier to be overcome.

It was to be a mid-morning take-off, so I did not need to go to bed too early, but I did so nevertheless, fearing that I might have difficulty getting to sleep. Which indeed I did! Those 'what if' scenarios kept churning through my mind and although I tried to dispel them, they kept coming back. Another thought, indirectly related, was remembering how much I had been affected, as a boy, by reading about the last man to be killed on the Western Front, at a minute to the eleventh hour of the eleventh day of the eleventh month of 1918, when the Armistice came into force. *How could fate be so cruel?* I had thought – but it had been in that case and could be again. Nevertheless, eventually I fell asleep.

Next morning there was no hurry. I lingered over breakfast and then donned my Beedon suit, marching boots, webbing belt with revolver, dagger and water bottle attached, parachute harness, lifejacket, etc. On this occasion it was all done in a very leisurely fashion. *For the last time?* I wondered. In due course, a jeep, with Geoff already aboard, arrived and took us out to our aircraft. On this occasion it was NV.210 'W' (not our favourite – NE.705 'V' – which we had been flying in mostly of late). *Was this a bad omen?* I quashed this and many other thoughts that flitted through my mind with a mental admonishment that I must treat this trip like any other.

Whilst Geoff was running up the engines, I stowed my navigation instruments away, checked the intercom, switched on the W/T set, then swivelled my seat round and checked that the rear gun was securely mounted – routine actions I had carried out dozens of times before, but was now very conscious of doing.

As usual, I was still sitting, facing backwards, as Geoff taxied away and I gave a half wave, half salute to the ground crew. One or two of them would always wave back and at that moment I realised what a 'must do' ritual this had become over the last few months. I always felt that they must be thinking 'shall we ever see them again' and on this occasion the thought was even more pertinent. To-day my arm felt heavy as lead. We lined up on the runway and took off at 1105 hours in the rapidly increasing heat of the day. It was a relief to start climbing as we headed towards the Chin Hills.

I will not attempt to recall this trip in detail because the narrative would virtually be a carbon copy of that for the previous sortie on 10th November. I had this constant feeling of *déjà vu* as we flew over the hills, then down to low-level and across the central part of Burma, crossed the railway south of Yamethin, at virtually the same point as before, and the made the long climb back up to about 7,000 feet. We saw no targets of opportunity and it was, thankfully, almost boringly uneventful.

The weather was good, with sunshine and blue sky, broken by a scattering of cumulus clouds, which usually tended to build up in the afternoon. We pressed on over this beautiful wooded, hilly, borderland between Burma and Siam until we crossed the Salween. Somehow even the spectacular glimpse of that river in the bottom of the ravine didn't seem quite so breathtaking as it had when we passed over it for the first time 22 days previously. Maybe because this time it was not so unexpected. Eventually, we reached that broad grassland valley and flashed across the Bhayo to Changrai road. The road was deserted in both directions but this time we did not turn northwards towards Changrai but carried straight on, climbing slightly to clear the wooded hills on the far side.

We were now over unfamiliar territory and about as remote from base as we had ever been. Descending into the next shallow valley, we found the small town of Mung Phayao without any difficulty. It looked peaceful in the afternoon sun and there was no sign of any military presence. We followed the road, which was little more than a track, heading north. At some points the track ran alongside wooded areas and at first I felt a bit apprehensive because there might be concealed machine gun posts guarding it but, as we flew on, everywhere seemed so deserted we began to think there were no Japanese forces at all in the area. This seemed to be confirmed at the next town of Chienggam, where we saw no sign of Japanese military and nobody fired at us. As we continued, the road improved a bit as it curved round westward to Dheung. At this point, two other tracks led off north-east towards Mekong river, which formed the border with China, only about thirty miles distant, but we followed our road, which meandered round to the west until it joined the Bhayo–Changrai road, just a few miles south of the latter.

That was it. We had patrolled 55 miles of road, as briefed, and had seen nothing, except a couple of innocent-looking bullock carts, which we let be. The fuel situation dictated that we must now set course back to base. The long trip back was uneventful but I well remember one unique moment, not long after we had crossed the Salween river again and were over Burmese territory, when I looked at my watch and realised that my total operational hours to date had just passed 200. I had completed a tour, but we were still about two flying hours away from base. I was working overtime!

In due course we reached the edge of the plateau and descended to low-level to traverse central Burma. This meant another spell of low flying for Geoff, who must have been getting tired by now. He had been frustrated because we had not found any enemy presence or transport movements in Siam and had said that maybe we would find some targets of opportunity on the way back. We didn't. As we climbed over the Chin Hills for the last time (I thought) and sighted the landing strip at Chiringa, I felt a growing feeling of relief but also of weariness. We touched down at 1720, having been airborne for six hours and fifteen minutes. It was our longest trip to date and the furthest away from base we had ever been, but it was also one of our least effective sorties. We hadn't even fired our guns.

I was first out of the aircraft, as usual, and it was normal for at least the armourer and the rigger to greet me – the first to ask whether I had fired my gun and the second to ask if I was aware of having been hit by enemy fire – but on this occasion four or five of the ground crew crowded round me, shaking my hand and congratulating me on completing my tour. One of them actually asked for my autograph, which was the first (and last!) time in my life anybody has done that. I was quite taken aback, because I didn't know that they knew. By this time, Geoff had climbed out also and they began to congratulate him too, but he began to play it down, saying to them, "No, I haven't completed my tour yet. I'm still about an hour short and I am not sure what the position is. But Denny has definitely finished and won't have to fly again."

In reply, there was a chorus of words from them, to the effect that nobody would make him go on another operation for the sake of just one hour. Some doubts about this entered my mind but I was too weary to think about them. I hastened to my basha to get out of my flying gear and over to the mess for dinner. It was around 1830 hours and suddenly hunger reminded me that I had been on a flight of over six hours with nothing to eat but a bar of chocolate and swigs of water from my water bottle.

Unusually, none of my closest friends and roommates, Tubby, China and Hoppy was about in our basha or the Mess. Tubby was in hospital, Hoppy was at briefing for a night operation (night operations were rare) and I don't remember why China was not around. After dinner, I was so weary I went straight to bed in our empty room. It just had not yet sunk in that I had finished my tour.

But it was a different story next morning! Our Bearer woke me with a mug of tea, as usual, at around 0700 hours and immediately I was overwhelmed by a wonderful feeling of relief as it finally sunk in. *I had survived a tour of operations!* As I went over to the Mess for breakfast, I really felt as though I was walking on air. I came back and sat on the veranda for a while in a state of euphoria.

But it did not last for long…

Around mid-morning Geoff came to my basha. He was looking rather glum and got straight to the point.

"I'm only about forty minutes short of my total," he said, "but the CO has ruled that I must do another trip, although you will not have to go Denny. In fact, he has specifically told me I must not ask you to do so." He went on to explain that he had come to ask for my opinion of two NCO navigators who were temporarily without pilots and might be willing to fly with him. He began to ask me questions about them. I did not know them very well but, anyway, my mind was not on them. I had received a sledgehammer blow that knocked me off cloud nine into a slough of despond. Geoff and I had done 50 sorties together. We had a good relationship in the air and the fact that we had survived was in no small measure due to his good airmanship. In my heart I knew that there was no way I could let him go on his last trip with a navigator who was a stranger to him. Equally, in my mind I knew that there was no way I could face the stress of doing a second 'last trip'. That surely would not just be tempting fate – it would be *taunting* fate!

While this heart/mind turmoil was going on, my mouth, seemingly independently, said, "I think I should come with you Geoff. Surely it would be alright with the CO if I volunteered?"

Geoff's face lit up somewhat as he said, "I really would feel happier if you came but I will have to go and ask the CO whether it's OK." He went away, leaving me sitting there – numb. I couldn't believe what I had just done. I had actually *volunteered* to do another trip!

Within half an hour Geoff was back. He told me that the CO had agreed that I could go and then he added what he called the 'good news'. We would be flying the very next day and he would see me in the briefing room this afternoon. Normally crews in 'B' Flight flew in strict rotation but the CO had authorised that we could fly 'out of turn' so that Geoff could complete his tour as soon as possible, instead of having to wait two or three days. As I walked over to the Briefing Room that afternoon, I once more had the feeling that I was being rushed into my last trip (albeit for the second time!)

without having time to come to terms with it. I felt apprehensive as I entered the briefing but all this changed when I got details of where we were going and learned that we would accompany another aircraft from 'A' Flight.

Our brief was simply to search for targets of opportunity within the area bounded by 19° to 21° N and 94° to 96° E. I felt some feeling of relief because this was the central area of Burma that I was most familiar with and it would be a more normal trip of three or four hours' duration. Secondly, the crew of the other aircraft were F/O Russell and his navigator F/O Spooner, who were on their first operational flight. It had been the policy on the squadron that, wherever possible, a crew on their first sortie would be accompanied by a more experienced crew. However, this would be the first time since the squadron had started flying Beaufighters at the beginning of the year that a crew on their first sortie were accompanied by a crew on their very last one.

The fact that we would, in a sense, be 'showing them the ropes' gave us some feeling of responsibility and on the way back from the briefing room I remember Geoff saying, "We shall have to do this one by the book." He meant flying really low, weaving at places where experience had showed it was advisable, crisscrossing rivers and railways rather than flying straight along them and warning them if they were straying too near known flack hotspots and so on. Moreover, in my case, being extra vigilant in looking out for fighters and keeping track of exactly where we were at all times. This all helped me to dispel any last trip jitters such as I had felt on my first 'last trip'!

The next morning, the 4th December, I got up late, as we were not due to take off until the afternoon. After lunch I donned my flying gear, again in a leisurely manner, in contrast to the many (52, in fact) previous occasions when I had done this by the flickering light of a hurricane lamp, while trying not to wake my two roommates. So many of our sorties had been pre-dawn take-offs.

We took off at 1325 hours in, I was pleased find, our favoured aircraft – NE.705 'V' – and were followed by F/O Russell in an 'A' Flight aircraft – NV.114 'M'. We kept together over the hills but once down at low-level we spread well apart to give ourselves a better chance of seeing enemy movements, although Geoff did ask me to try and keep them in sight all the time. I was kept busy, concentrating on what I was doing and found that I really was treating it 'like any other trip'. It was not particularly eventful. We patrolled the road from just north of Allanmyo to Sattwa and then went across to Kidaunggan and followed another road until we reached the railway at Tatkon. No movements were seen. Nor was anything seen on the railway as we followed it for some distance northward. We dropped some leaflets at Yamethin and then turned towards the Irrawaddy. On the river near Sinbaunge a number of small river craft were seen. F/O Russell strafed seven sampans and one large kistie.

We flew back together over the hills and landed at Chiringa, having been airborne for 3 hours and 45 minutes. It was their first sortie and this time it really was our last. As we got out of the aircraft, this time it was Geoff who the ground crew fell upon with congratulations. For me it was a bit of an anti-climax, but still a wonderful feeling. By the time I had changed and freshened up, it was dinner time. That evening I was elated and I sank gin after gin, *ad infinitum*.

After I surfaced, around mid-morning next day, I found myself once more sitting in the sun on our veranda, sipping a mug of char. I was back on cloud nine, for the second time in 72 hours, only this time, with my flying hours totalling 206, I *knew* that nobody was going to expect me to fly on operations again – at least for the next six months of my rest period.

I fact, although I did not know it at the time, I was never to fly in a Beaufighter again.

~ END ~

Addendum: Some Memorable Moments

A very scary night

Soon after we had moved to Chiringa and were beginning to get things organised, there occurred a rather frightening incident. At dusk, just as we were due to go over to the Mess for dinner, the unmistakable sound of automatic weapons being fired rang out in the still night air. There were several prolonged bursts, together with some sporadic rifle fire. As can be imagined, this caused considerable alarm and consternation, because the airstrip was completely undefended and had been so since the end of 1943, when the RAF had been forced to abandon it. But at this stage of the war, the nearest Japanese forces were now about 50 miles away in the jungle area of Buthidaung, which formed a bit of a natural barrier. The nearest British army garrison was 20 miles away.

The CO made contact with this garrison by land line to try and find out what was going on. All they could tell him was that they too had heard the firing but they didn't know what was happening. They had a patrol out but had lost contact with it. They were preparing to send out a second patrol and meanwhile, as a precaution, they suggested that we should treble the guards on the aircraft and issue arms to all personnel. We aircrew, of course, had our revolvers but these would be no match for automatic weapons.

Imaginations ran wild. Was a Japanese patrol stealthily creeping up on us at this very moment? There was nowhere to shelter or hide. We extinguished hurricane lamps and sat on our beds, ears strained for any telltale sounds. It was very, very scary.

The night dragged on. Everyone was jumpy and nobody wanted to sleep. Then, at about three o'clock in the morning, news came of another telephone call from the Army garrison saying that it had been a false alarm. Apparently, in the darkness, one section of the patrol had mistakenly opened fire on the other.

Needless to say, there was great relief all round.

A Near Disaster

One day, returning from an otherwise uneventful patrol at dawn, we suddenly came across a large but isolated building. Part of it was two storeys high, which was unusual. We concluded that it was an Inn or 'Doss House' because there were four military vehicles and a jeep parked outside. There was nobody about as Geoff quickly swung round to make an attack. With one sustained burst from the 20mm cannon three of the vehicles burst into flames and the fourth was smouldering.

As quickly as he could, Geoff swung round to make a second attack to get the jeep as well. Meanwhile, a dozen or so soldiers were streaming out and gazing in horror and bewilderment at the scene. Some of the vehicles were still exploding and I don't think they heard our Beaufighter coming in for a second attack.

I was facing forwards and along the top of the fuselage I got a brief glimpse of a Japanese officer, who appeared on the steps at the door. He was an absolute stereotype – jackboots, knee-breeches, sword, horn-rimmed glasses – the lot. He seemed quite oblivious to the fact that Geoff was about to blow him and his jeep to Kingdom Come. Geoff opened fire.

Behind the Inn there were some trees and on the first attack he had to pull up very sharply to avoid them. For this second attack the line of approach was different, more towards the left-hand end of the building, where there were several taller trees. I thought that Geoff's burst of cannon fire was being prolonged just a few milliseconds too long. I could see the danger.

"*Watch out for those bloody trees!*" I yelled at the top of my voice, in order to be heard above the din of the cannons.

He stopped firing instantly and pulled back on the control column as hard as he could. Even so, we 'mushed' into the top of the tallest one and I watched as the port engine propeller did a pruning job. Twigs and leaves flew everywhere but we just made it. Geoff said nothing for a while then remarked, "It's a good job you warned me when you did, Denny." He knew he had made a near fatal misjudgement, but for me it was already in the past.

As we left the scene, we noted that barely 300 yards further on the trees came right down to the roadside. If only the Japs had taken the trouble to park their four vehicles amongst those trees we would probably have flown by without noticing them. I imagine it had been dark when they arrived and they no doubt had planned to leave shortly after daybreak. What they hadn't planned for was a visit by 'Whispering Death'.

Back at base there was evidence of foliage in the engine cowling and elsewhere, which prompted one wag amongst the ground crew to comment, "See you've been gardening again, Sir!"

The Blue and Gold Dress

Much of the time we flew really low, so as to avoid detection as far as possible. This demanded a high degree of concentration on Geoff's part, to avoid hitting any obstructions on the ground, but in my case, apart from keeping track of where we were, I was able just to observe. It is amazing the amount of detail you can take in within just a few seconds. One day we were flying across a field towards a fairly high hedge, behind which was a road that we wanted to check out, when we were quite surprised to see a smart-looking pony and trap trotting briskly along the road.

They had obviously not heard our Beaufighter, with its phenomenally silent approach, particularly at low-level, until it whooshed over them. I saw a woman, who was dressed in what must have been traditional Burmese costume, get up and start hitting the driver's arm to make him stop. Meanwhile, her companion, a man, opened the little door at the back and then fumbled with the fold-down step. But even before the pony had halted, the woman, panic-stricken and without waiting for the step to be lowered, either jumped or fell onto the road, followed by the man. They picked themselves up and ran about six yards before throwing themselves into a ditch. The driver seemed bewildered, as if he didn't know what had happened and the pony, instead of bolting, just stood obediently, awaiting instructions.

I wanted to call out to them "Don't panic. We won't hurt you. We are not at war with the Burmese people," as we flew on. I have often wondered if the woman hurt herself. Did she get mud on that beautiful dress? I shall never know.

Later I mentioned the incident at de-briefing, because it showed that there was still some degree of normality, at least amongst the more well-to-do Burmese, allowing them to attend social functions, provided they collaborated with the Japanese. The debriefing officer was old Smithy, noted for his lack of humour, but he agreed to make a note of it. He then asked me to describe the dress. Apart from adding that it had a very voluminous skirt and an intricate blue and gold pattern I could not add more. I did suggest that if navigators were required to be experts in Burmese *haute couture* then it should be included in their training, but I think that remark was lost on him!

Brush with the USAAF

One day, returning from a long but rather uneventful patrol, our track back to base took us about four miles south of the town of Kalewa on the Chindwin River. We had already begun the long climb to get over the Chin Hills, even before crossing the river, because the mountains rose quite quickly at this point. I had just asked Geoff to edge a bit nearer to Kalewa, so that I could get a good look at the state of the pontoon bridge and report on it, but before we could do this I was surprised to see two ack-ack gun flashes from an area within the town, followed by two shell bursts quite a bit higher than us and on our starboard side. I could not believe they were firing at us, because we were out of their range, and I doubted they could see us anyway. I quickly took a look around, particularly back in the direction of Monywa, to make sure there were no Japanese fighters following us, but saw nothing. There was about sixth tenths scattered cumulus cloud over the hills, with blue sky visible above. My attention was mainly in the direction of Kalewa, until I happened to look southward and got such a shock, as the sky suddenly seemed to be full of aircraft. They had been obscured by the clouds. Geoff and I saw them at the same moment. We were climbing virtually on a collision course with at least 24 American B.25 Mitchell bombers, obviously on a bombing run to Kalewa.

Geoff had to decide very quickly what to do. To continue on our course and pass two or three hundred feet below them was unthinkable; those tensed-up, itchy-trigger-fingered US gunners would almost certainly think we were an enemy aircraft. Neither could he turn to starboard, for then we would run into the flak from Kalewa intended for the B.25s. He therefore decided to turn to port, in the opposite direction to the US aircraft, and dive like the clappers into a valley we could see below us. This way, we would get out of their range, both below and behind them, as quickly as possible.

However, even as he put the nose down, I was alarmed to see that they had a fighter escort, which emerged from behind a cloud, about a 1,000 feet above them.

Maybe they won't see us, I thought. But then, to my horror, the high speed of our dive, no doubt together with the high humidity in the valley, began to produce white vapour trails from our wingtips, which must have contrasted starkly with the dark green of the vegetation in the valley. I half expected a couple of the fighters to peel off and dive down after us, but they carried on in formation. Meanwhile, every second we were getting further out of range, below and behind the B.25s and soon began to level off in the relative safety of the valley.

However, almost immediately I had to warn Geoff that this valley was getting narrower and that on my map it appeared to have a dead end. He turned, but in order to keep out of the way of the B.25s he started to climb, quite steeply, completing two full spirals, with engines labouring and drinking up our fuel reserves, until we gained sufficient height to clear the first ridge of hills on our westward side and could resume our track back to base, across the main mountain range.

At debriefing, after we got back, Geoff was angry because the Intelligence Officer had not warned us about this impending raid. All he said was that the Americans had warned him, but only about an hour after we had taken off. They had considered recalling us, but believed that by this time we would be out of W/T range.

At this time the Japanese were in retreat over the Chin Hills and their route back would be through Kalewa, but there were stubborn pockets of resistance at places like Tiddim, Kennedy Peak and Fort White and B25s of the USAAF 12th Bombardment Group were providing assistance by bombing. I have had access to some USAAF records on microfilm but the records, although quite detailed, are not clear and I have not been able to establish the date of this particular air raid. It may have been on 2nd September. On this date, Kalewa was an alternative target, to be attacked if the primary target was obscured by cloud, and it may be that our Intelligence Officer had not anticipated this.

Geoff's Nightmare

About mid-August, when 'A' and 'B' Flights of 211 squadron were still the only occupants of the site at Chiringa, and as yet there was still no RT equipment installed in the flying control hut, Geoff and I were briefed for a sortie that required us to arrive in the target area at first light. Accordingly, I had worked out that we would have to take-off at about 0320 hours when it would still be dark and we would need the flarepath to be lit.

The flarepath consisted of a row of about a dozen gooseneck flares burning kerosene. These were like large 'Aladdin's Lamps', suspended about three feet above the ground from hooks on iron rods. The flame burned from wicks, about an inch thick, that dangled down from the gooseneck. As can be imagined, they burned with smoky, flickering flames, casting eerie shadows, but at least they formed a straight line to guide the pilot for take-off.

The flares had already been lit as we were driven out to our aircraft, which was conveniently parked close to the north end of the runway, but Geoff seemed concerned about the weather. Low stratus cloud and drizzle was causing poor visibility but he decided we ought to 'have a go'. We got aboard, ran up the engines and moved out onto the runway, where we stopped for a moment, with engines idling.

"O.K. for take-off Denny?" he said, as usual.

"Yes," I replied, but curiously he did not open the throttles immediately but remained stationary for few moments more. Meanwhile, my attention was taken up by a jeep, driving fast (or rather, as fast as was possible with dimmed out headlights) along the bumpy ground beside the flarepath.

At that moment there was an anguished cry of '*Bloody Hell!*' from Geoff, as a Beaufighter, taking off in the wrong direction, whooshed overhead, missing us by inches. Our aircraft rocked from wingtip to wingtip from the slipstream. Had it hit us, I would never have known what had happened, but for Geoff, as he told me later, it had been a nightmare.

He had delayed take-off for a few moments because, in the eerie, flickering light of those flares, he thought he could see something moving on the runway. Too late, he identified this as the glow from the exhausts of another Beaufighter approaching head-on at full take-off power. To move our aircraft out of the way he would have to open the throttle on one engine to pull it round off the runway but it would take about five seconds for an engine to develop enough torque to do this… and he hadn't got five seconds. Consequently, he had to sit there and watch, helplessly, as it approached, knowing that there was absolutely no action he could take to get out of its way. It missed us by inches.

After this experience, Geoff said he was going to cancel the sortie and taxied back to the dispersal point. As we got out, I could see that he was still trembling, both from shock and rage at the utterly irresponsible action of that 'A' Flight pilot.

The near collision had, of course, been witnessed by the 'B' Flight ground crew and as we all drove up to the other end of the runway we heard the other Beaufighter come in and land.

Geoff told us all to stay where we were while he strode off to 'have words' with the other pilot.

Raised voices, indeed a right slanging match, rang out in the still night air. Eventually the shouting died down and after about 15 minutes Geoff returned to the jeep. He addressed the ground crew, saying that he and the other pilot had put the incident down to a 'misunderstanding' and asked them not to discuss it further, but he did turn to me and say, "Is that alright with you, Denny? You were nearly killed too."

Of course, I knew who the other pilot was and I must admit that I hesitated for a minute. As I sat there in that jeep I felt I held that pilot's future career in my hand. But then I thought that Geoff's experience had been much more horrific than mine and if he was prepared to let it go at that then so should I.

"OK," I said, and we all went off back to bed.

Later that morning, in private, Geoff did tell me a bit more about the mental state of that pilot, which partly explained, but did not excuse, what I regarded as an unauthorised take-off.

Epilogue

During the period of my operational flying on 211 Squadron, from mid-April to the beginning of December 1944, nine crews were lost from 'B' Flight and about the same number from 'A' Flight. These comrades died believing, as we all did, that they were fighting to help drive the Japanese invaders out of Burma and hopefully to introduce some form of democratic rule.

The first objective was achieved but over 60 years later democratic rule has yet to arrive in Burma.

In 1945, even before I had left India, I remember reading newspaper reports that Clement Attlee, Prime Minister of the newly-formed Labour government, with what seemed to me to be almost indecent haste and pious wringing of anti-colonial socialist hands, announced that he was giving Burma back to the Burmese. Unfortunately he was not too fussy about which of 'The Burmese' he handed it to. In next to no time, a Military Junta had seized power and has ruled ever since, often with brutal force against dissenters.

I returned home and was demobilised in June 1946. I concentrated on re-establishing myself in my career as a Development Engineer and tried to push Burma out of my mind, but from time to time I read disturbing reports in the papers about atrocities committed by the Junta, particularly against the peoples in the north.

In later years I heard about that wonderfully brave Burmese woman, Aung San Suu Kyi, who, being dedicated to non violence, was campaigning for democratic rule. In 1990 her Opposition Party won a landslide victory and she was elected as their leader, but the Junta promptly declared the election to be void and placed her under house arrest, where she still remains, at the time of writing.

So what did I learn from my participation in this war?

That war is futile, that it seldom solves anything and that it often creates further problems.

Since middle age, I have been a pacifist.

Dennis Spencer
February 2009

The Author, photographed in 2003.

APPENDIX ~ Log of My 51 Operational Sorties with Geoff Vardigans as pilot

(Highlighted entries have been expanded into full length narratives in the book).

Date	A/C No	I/D	T/O time	Duration (h-min)	Operation
(Operating from BHATPARA)					
1/5/44	LZ.479	O	0800	4-40	Target. BHAMO-SIKAW-MONGMIT-KYAUPYU roads: Geoff's first op. Accompanied by 'W' with a more experienced crew (F/O Haakenson & F/S Ferguson). Not much seen on roads. Bus and a Lorry attacked.
3/5/44	LZ.153	N	0730	0-45	Attempted ops. but returned with engine trouble. Geoff made a 'heavy' landing causing slight damage to the undercarriage.
4/5/44	LZ.479	O	0530	3-25	Target. SAGAING to MONYWA road and rail: No movements seen. Bridge at ALLAGAPPA attacked with R.P. Bullock carts, some sampans on the Chindwin strafed en route.
6/5/44	NE.298	V	0630	3-25	Target. SAGAING-PAKOKKU area: Strafed railway wagons at KYNHMON, bullock carts on road between ALLAGAPPA and WUNBYE and several rivercraft on the Irrawaddy. LZ.479 (F/S Bell & F/S Nash) was in the same area. We saw them heading back towards the Hills. They were flying straight and level at about 300 ft but did not appear to be in trouble nor did they seem to see us. This aircraft failed to return.
10/5/44	NE.298	V	0615	4-45	Target. TAUNGUP to DALET road: No movements seen on road but small bridge at SABAYIN attacked with R.P. Several sampans strafed.
12/5/44	NE.298	V	0800	3-55	Target. SAGAING-SWEBO-WUNTHO road and rail: Commenced patrol at ONDAW. Attacked canal bridge near WETLET with R.P. Destroyed another small bridge further north. Patrolled railway up to WUNTHO, no movements seen.
13/5/44	NE.298	V	1336	4-10	'Scrambled' take off, together with NE.288 (F/O Stevens & F/O Parker), to fly to CHITTAGONG for briefing. Airborne from CHITTAGONG at 1445 hours. Task. To search for and attack a concentration of barges reported in the coastal area near TAUNGUP. Searched creeks and waterways in the specified area for about 40 minutes but found no barges. Hit several times by LMG fire. Before leaving the area we both fired full salvos of R.P. into the garrison town of TAUNGUP in an area thought to be an M.T. park and storage dump.

Date	A/C No	I/D	T/O time	Duration (h-min)	Operation
17/5/44	NE.713	Z	0330	5-05	Target. TAUNGUP PASS: Together with NE.317 X (F/S Gamlin & W/O Mearns) we flew over the sea to the coastal end of the Pass. In spite of low cloud and poor visibility we followed the road a short way up it to a point where it disappeared into cloud ahead. A column of military vehicles literally emerged from cloud with headlights on. We each made two attacks, manoeuvring in the confined space, setting about a dozen on fire before we had to retire back towards the coast.
21/5/44	NE.713	Z	0645	3-35	Target. Irrawaddy river from CHAUK to ALLANMYO: Strafed a number of rivercraft at ZIBYUBIN, KAYUKYE and PINWA. 15 kisties, 9 sampans and 6 sandoways destroyed or damaged.
25/5/44	NE.298	V	0605	4-15	(Just before take-off we were instructed to land at FENI on return). Target. THAZI to PYINMANA railway: Strafed rolling stock on sidings along route. Attacked occupied locomotive shelter at TATKON with two pairs of R.P. Hit by LMG fire at YAMETHIN. Landed at FENI 1215 hours.
(Operating from FENI)					
29/5/44	NE.298	V	0755	3-10	Target. KALEWA-YE-U-MONYWA roads: Together with NE.288 O (F/S Williams & Sgt Gollop) patrolled from KALEWA to YE-U and then to just N. of MONYWA but no movements seen on roads. Attacked 3 rolling stock on siding at KANBYA and station buildings at SEGYI.
31/5/44	NE.298	V	0800	2-20	Target. CHINDWIN river N. of Lat.23° to MYINGYON. Although we got over the Chin Hills there was 10/10ths low cloud over the target area and we returned to base.
5/6/44	NE.298	V	0816	3-50	Target. TANGON to SAGAING railway: Together with 'K' (F/S Thomson & F/S Whale) attacked bridge at MANDAUNGHLA with R.P. and strafed factory at KETKA. Loco shelter and buildings hit with R.P. at ZIGON.
8/6/44	NE.366	T	0534	4-05	Task. Escort incoming convoy of 5 ships and 4 escort vessels from reported position 21° 20′N, 91° 35′E to, 21° - 53′N, 91° 38′E for two hours: Relief Beaufighter did not arrive and we stayed with the convoy for another hour.
10/6/44	NE.298	V	0347	4-20	Task. Opportunity targets in central Burma: 2 M.T. destroyed, 2 M.T. damaged. Also 30 ft. motor vessel strafed at SAGAING.
11/6/44	NE.298	V	0800	4-50	Task. Patrol the Arakan ccast down to GWA BAY: No movements seen but attacked a Pagoda and other building, believed to be observation posts, on CHEDUBA ISLAND.

Date	A/C No	IID	T/O time	Duration (h-min)	Operation
15/6/44	NE.317	X	0755	3-45	Target. Irrawaddy river from CHAUK to ALLANMYO: Low cloud and rain over much of the river but managed to attack and damage 10 kisties. On returning over the hills found that the weather had clamped down over the whole of the Arakan region. Our base at Feni and also the airstrips at Cox's Bazaar and Chittagong were all unserviceable. We managed to get down through cloud and locate Chittagong but on attempting an emergency landing on the partially flooded runway in a violent storm the port undercarriage leg gave way and we swung off the runway into flooded paddy fields. We narrowly missed a head on collision with an American B.25 also making an emergency landing, without permission, from the opposite direction. We eventually got back to base by train!
19/6/44	LZ.483	M	0650	3-30	Task. Patrol HUNTERS BAY area: Patrolled the numerous creeks and waterways in the HUNTERS BAY area south of AKYAB but no movements seen except a working Elephant stacking logs. (Working Elephants were officially 'military targets' but we decided not to attack it or report it).
22/6/44	NE.298	V	0800	2-30	Target. Communications in central Burma and M.T. dump at PADAUNG: Bad weather forced us to return to base and this sortie was abortive.
25/6/44	LZ.483	M	1320	3-15	Target. PYINGAING to KALEWA road: Spotted about 50 vehicles, mostly three tonners, strung out along the road near KALEWA. Rain and low cloud in the area hampered attacks but 3 vehicles were destroyed and about 6 badly damaged.
27/6/44	LZ.483	M	0700	4-00	Task. Patrol the Arakan coast south of AKYAB: No movements seen but strafed an observation post on RAMREE ISLAND.
29/6/44	LZ.483	M	0905	3-20	Target. Irrawaddy and Chindwin rivers between ALON and CHAUK: Strafed a number of rivercraft. 6 kisties and 36 sampans destroyed or damaged. Also strafed bashas at MYITCHE which appeared to be occupied by military personnel.
2/7/44	LZ.483	M	0805	2-30	Target. Coastal waterways, MYEBON to TAUNGUP: Bad weather along this part of the coast caused sortie to be aborted and we returned to base.
5/7/44	NE.298	V	0940	3-40	Task. Patrol coastal region MINBYA to TAUNGUP also Recce. M.T. park at KYWEGU: 2 sampans strafed but nothing else seen in waterways. No M.T.seen at KYWEGU but bashas attacked with R.P. Leaflets dropped.

Date	A/C No	I/D	T/O time	Duration (h-min)	Operation
8/7/44	NE.298	V	0445	5-10	Target. PROME to OKKAN railway. Also check reported activity at HENZADA branch line and ferry crossing: No movements seen on HENZADA branch. Joined main line to PROME just N. of LETPADAN. Attacked oil pipeline but were hit by a heavy AA shell which passed right through fuselage without exploding. Damage to hydraulic system - all fluid lost. Returned to base by coastal route. Crash landed at base (no undercarriage or flaps). Little damage on landing but aircraft was written off because of severe damage to fuselage caused by the shell.
9/7/44	NE.713	Z	1510	-35	Flew this aircraft to our new base at CHIRINGA. Weather poor-lot of rain and low cloud.
(Operating from CHIRINGA)					
15/7/44	LX.938	D	1345	1-00	Target. PYU to PINMANA railway: Sortie attempted but unable to get up through 10/10ths cloud over the Hills.
					(On leave from 17/7/44 to 6/8/44)
10/8/44	NE.464	V	0440	3-30	Task. Any communications targets S. of Lat.23° N Together with LX.938 D (P/O Macdonald & W/O Freeman) attacked one 3 ton truck at PYINGAING and two more at THITYAGAUK. Six sampans strafed on Chindwin S. of MONYWA. 400 leaflets dropped S. of MONYWA.
13/8/44	LX.938	W	1038	4-30	Task. Any communications targets in area 23°.N and 94° to 96° E. Patrolled PAKOKKU-SAGAING-SWEBO-MONYWA regions but no movements seen. Leaflets dropped.
16/8/44	NE.752	X	1055	3-50	Target. KYAIKTO to MOULMEIN road/rail and any shipping in the GULF of MARTABAN: Set off, together with 5 other aircraft, down the coast route but as we turned to cross the delta at GWA BAY we developed severe vibration in the port engine and turned back. NE.366 T (F/O Stevens & F/O Parker) decided to escort us back. At one stage ditching looked imminent and we jettisoned R.P. near FOUL ISLAND, but by reducing power Geoff 'nursed' the engine and we made it back to base.
18/8/44	NE.646	V	0915	5-10	Target. KYAIKTO to MOULMEIN road/rail: Nothing seen along the section we patrolled. Leaflets dropped. On returning over the delta we came across a large (c.130 ft.) river steamer under way in a navigable waterway near SHWELAUNG. Attacked and hit with two R.P. Circled for second attack but did not fire. Steamer was listing and being run aground on to sandbank. Few Japanese soldiers and many people wading ashore. Went round again to note more details but hit by small arms fire and left. Attacked a small Tug seen nearby at KYUNGON.

Date	A/C No	IID	T/O time	Duration (h-min)	Operation
2/9/44	NE.646	V	0555	3-15	Task. Any communications targets in area 21° to 23° N and 94 to 96° E: Patrolled roads and the railway between KYAUKSE and HANZA but no movements seen. Leaflets dropped at stations and villages and also in the KYAUKPADAUNG AREA.
5/9/44	NE.752	X	1030	6-45	Target. Small convoy of four 1000 ton vessels reported to be sheltering in YE Harbour on the far side of the Gulf of Martaban: Accompanied by three other aircraft we all reached YE together but the ships were gone. R.P.'s were fired at jetties and buildings. Two 40 ft barges strafed in the mouth of the Ye estuary. Factory and Rice mill attacked at PYAPON.
12/9/44	NE.646	V	0510	3-50	Task. Any communications targets on road/rail link from MANDALAY to GOKTEIK: Together with aircraft 'B' (F/O Moffat & W/O Morris) we patrolled both the road and railway. Attacked 2 saloon cars, 2 three ton MT, 1 locomotive and also 1 kistie on river near Maymyo. 450 leaflets dropped S. of Mandalay.
14/9/44	NE.740	Z	0930	4-25	Target. Rivercraft in the delta region from KYAUGIN to HENZADA. Also report on state of bridges at LETPAN,LAMU and LABYIN: Together with aircraft 'G' (P/O Shippen & Sgt.Oblein) we covered the area and found many targets. We attacked about 100 sampans and small craft. Also a 60 ft kistie. 1350 leaflets dropped. No bridge seen at LETPAN, but those at LAMU and LABYIN still standing.
18/9/44	LZ.229	H	1000	2-45	Target. Road from NAMHSAN to LASHIO: Reached the area but rain and low cloud made it impossible to follow this tortuous road through the hills more than a few miles. Aborted operation and returned to base.
21/9/44	NE.540	Z	0620	5-10	Task. Opportunity targets - BASSEIN-HENZADA-LETPADAN southwards: Patrolled railway and roads in the area but no movements seen. Attacked a 20 ft rivercraft on the Irrawaddy at ZALUN. Attacked the oil pipeline between LETPADAN and THARRAWADDY. Saw a fighter in the distance, in the direction of Mingladon, as we left the area.
26/9/44	NV.210	W	0615	6-05	Task. Shipping recce. in GULF OF MARTABAN: Dropped 340 Burmese News Sheets on villages as we crossed the Irrawaddy delta on the way. Crossed the Gulf and patrolled off the enemy coast in the region of the mouths of the Salween river near Moulmein. No shipping seen except a few fishing boats off BILUGYUN ISLAND. Returning across the Gulf we saw two Japanese fighters over Elephant Point, which lay on our route home. To avoid them we had to make a detour to the SW and round the S end of the Delta to Pagoda Point before turning northwards up the coast home.

186 ~ *Looking Backwards Over Burma*

Date	A/C No	I/D	T/O time	Duration (h-min)	Operation
					(On leave from 29/9/44 to 17/10/44)
23/10/44	NE.705	V	0600	6-25	Task. Shipping recce. GULF of MARTABAN off MOULMEIN: Together with aircraft 'E' (F/S Birch & F/O Carter) we patrolled the sea area off Moulmein but no shipping seen except one apparently derelict coaster which was strafed anyway.
27/10/44	NE.705	V	0410	3-55	Target. Railway PYU to PIYNMANA: Arrived at first light and patrolled line but nothing seen.
1/11/44	NE.705	V	0605	3-45	Target. PYU to YEDASHE road/rail: Heavy rain and low cloud covered the area. Instead we patrolled road from PROME to ALLENMYO. Several bullock cart trains strafed. No movements seen on the Irrawwady.
5/11/44	NE.705	V	0555	4-45	Target. BASSEIN to HENZADA river and delta waterways W of the IRRAWADDY: We attacked 4 paddy gigs and 5 kisties S. of HENZADA. Also 1 country craft, 2 kisties and 2 sampans in the area of KYWEDON.
8/11/44	NE.705	V	0320	5-40	Target. MOKPALIN to MOULMEIN railway: Patrolled the section MARTABAN to KYAIKKATHA but no movements seen. Dropped leaflets at HNINPALE and also at stations along the LETPADAN to PROME railway on the way back.
10/11/44	NV.256	Y	1015	6-10	Target. CHIENGRAI to LAMPANG road: Together with NV.210 W (F/O Stayman & W/O Hopkins). Attacked 2 steam road rollers and some bullock carts. Leaflets dropped near CHIENGRAI and BHAYHO and also near CHAUK on way back.
15/11/44	NV.114	M	0715	1-35	Target NAMHSAN to LASHIO road: After about 40 mins. developed excessive oil temperature and vibration in one engine. Returned to base and later took another aircraft.
15/11/44	NV.256	Y	0930	4-40	Patrolled road from NAMHSAN to LASHIO but no movements seen. Dropped leaflets at MOGOK, YAMETHIN, and MAGWE on way back.
19/11/44	NE.705	V	1325	3-30	(Form 540 page missing so I do not know where we went, but Form 541 records no movements seen.)
23/11/44	NE.705	V	1000	3-40	Target. Area bounded by 20° to 22°N and 95° to 97°E: Patrolled roads and railways MAGWE-YAMETHIN-KYIDAUNGGAN-SATTWA-ALLANMYO. No movements seen. Leaflets dropped.
28/11/44	NE.705	V	1855	4-15	(This was a night operation) Target. SITKWIN to TAIKKYI road and rail: A convoy of vehicles with lights on was seen and attacked near SITKWIN. The first 3 or 4 were set on fire but when those following put out their lights further attacks were not effective. We searched the area for about 15 mins. then followed the line of the railway down to TAIKKYI but no more lights or movements were seen. Leaflets were dropped just N. of LETPADAN.

Date	A/C No	I/D	T/O time	Duration (h-min)	Operation
2/12/44	NV.210	W	1105	6-15	Target. MUANG PHOYAO to CHIENGRAI ROAD: This was a lesser road even further E. than the one we had previously been to. We patrolled it up to just S. of CHIENGRAI but no movements were seen. This trip took my total beyond 200 flying hours and officially completed my tour. Geoff was about 2 hours short but it was thought that this would be ignored. (The next day he was told that he would have to do another trip and should find another navigator to go with him as he must not ask me to do so. However I volunteered and thus I did a second 'last trip'.)
4/12/44	NE.705	V	1325	3-45	Target. Area bounded by 19° to 21°N and 94° to 96°E. We were accompanied by NV.114 M with a new crew (F/O Russell & F/O Spooner) as No.2. Patrolled road from 12 miles N of ALLANMYO to SATTWA. No movements seen on road from KYIDAUNGGAN to TATKON or on railway from TATKON to YAMETHIN. Leaflets dropped at YAMETHIN. 7 sampans and 1 kistie were strafed on the Irrawaddy just S of SINBAUNGWE. This trip completed Geoff's tour.

Notes On Aircrew Log Books

RAF aircrews kept Flying Log Books, recording dates, flying times, type of aircraft flown, etc. There was a column for remarks on the purpose or nature of the flight, but in wartime, during our operational flying on No.211 Squadron, we were told not enter details of where we had been or what we had done. Instead, we just had to write 'Operations'. This was said to be for security reasons, just as we were not allowed to keep diaries. It was pointed out that, in any case, the log books would remain the property of the Air Ministry and we would not be allowed to keep them.

In the event, however, it proved to be very easy to reclaim them a few years after the war, simply by writing to the Air Ministry and I have mine amongst my memorabilia. Some fifty years later, when I decided to write some memoirs of my wartime experiences flying over Burma, I found that whilst I could still remember some of the sorties in great detail, there were blanks in my memory regarding others. I wished I had disobeyed instructions, as some navigators did, and written more details in my log book.

However, as a result of enquiries, I discovered that the squadron ORBs (Operational Record Books, which they were required to keep when engaged in operations against an enemy) were still in existence at the RAF Records Office at Hayes. Furthermore, around 1975 they were freed from the secrecy laws, have been photographed on microfilm, and were available for public scrutiny in the Public Records Office at Kew. With the help of a researcher, Miss E. Wilson, I now have photocopies of the relevant pages for the period that my pilot and I were engaged on operational flying.

These ORB's, together with my own log book and memories, have enabled me to compile this complete log of the 51 operational sorties flown by my pilot, the late Geoffrey V. Vardigans, with me as his Navigator.

The role of the squadron at this time was that of interdiction. This involved sorties deep into Japanese occupied territory, mostly at low level, to patrol specified sections of roads, railways and rivers to deter the enemy from using them during daylight hours.

Notes On Low Level Map Reading

When I sought out the acting Navigating Officer, I found that I knew him, as he had been at navigation school with me in Canada. He had already been on several sorties and was able to give me some advice.

"Best forget most of what we were taught," he said with a laugh. "The majority of trips are at low level with your pilot frequently taking evasive action. It's not practical to use charts for plotting or to use the normal log forms, and in any case we don't have any charts or log forms!"

"So you don't try to keep an 'air plot going then?" I said. "Goodness no!" he replied. "Plot tracks and make measurements on topographical maps and use a knee pad for jotting down times and other observations."

The RAF manual on Air Navigation (AP.1234) then extant devoted only one quarter of a page to 'Low-Flying over Land' and this was mainly about which techniques were **not** practical.

We were issued with maps of 1:1,000,000 scale and four of them, each about 26 in. wide by 19 in. high, covered the main area over which we normally flew. To facilitate handling them in the navigator's cockpit I stuck the four of

Bibliography

Beaufighters over Burma by David J. Innes, 1985, Blandford Press.

Mission to Burma: the Story of 177 Squadron by Fred W. Burton, 1991, published privately by the author.

Silently into the Midst of Things – 177 Squadron Royal Air Force in Burma by Atholl Sutherland Brown, 1997, The Book Guild Ltd.

Long Sunset by Anthony Montague Brown, 1995, Cassells Publishers Ltd. (Chapter 3 refers to the author's time as a pilot on 211 Squadron).

The Forgotten Air Force: The RAF in the War Against Japan 1941-1945 by Air Commodore Henry Probert, 1995, Brassey's, London.